75 HARD

A TACTICAL GUIDE TO WINNING
THE WAR WITH YOURSELF

ANDY FRISELLA

TABLE OF CONTENTS

DISCLAIMER

BEFORE YOU READ THIS BOOK...

...It is **IMPERATIVE** that you understand the following:

This program is called 75Hard for a reason. Although the program is simple (meaning, it is not complicated), nothing about it is easy. Absolutely nothing. In order to complete it, you will be required to invest a lot of time and an enormous amount of physical, psychological, and emotional energy. For that reason, 75Hard is not for everyone. It is only for those who truly want to experience the benefits by embracing the program wholeheartedly. If that is not you, don't even bother turning the page. Return the book.

75Hard cannot be "customized" or "personalized" in any way. Every aspect of the program is designed to be intricately connected to every other aspect. Therefore, any change to the program, no matter how seemingly insignificant, makes it a completely different program. In order to experience the benefits of 75Hard, you must complete it to the letter. Anyone who compromises or deviates on any aspect of 75Hard cannot expect to experience the benefits.

In this book, you will be discouraged from "making excuses" and urged to "start right away." It's imperative to have the awareness if you are just making excuses trying to make it easier on yourself or if you truly cannot complete the program due to physical and/or mental health conditions. As with all programs that require physical exertion and/or exercise, **YOU SHOULD CONSULT YOUR PHYSICIAN OR OTHER HEALTH CARE PROFESSIONAL** before starting 75Hard. Do **NOT** start 75Hard if your physician or health care provider advises against it.

INTRODUCTION

Let me ask you a question to start off. If you were able to pay someone to multiply the traits below within you by 100x, what do you think the cost would be?

CONFIDENCE.

SELF-BELIEF.

SELF-ESTEEM.

DISCIPLINE.

DETERMINATION.

PERSEVERANCE.

GRIT.

I've asked hundreds of thousands of people that question again & again and they all answer the same way:

"I couldn't put a dollar value on it that would be high enough.
It would be priceless."

They are 1000 percent right…. & the reason it would be priceless is that together those things form the most valuable thing you can possibly possess for happiness & success.

It's the thing that will determine whether or not your relationships are healthy…

The thing that will determine whether or not you excel at your career…

The thing that will determine how much money you earn…

The thing that will determine whether or not you absolutely crush the biggest & most absurd goals you set for yourself…

The thing that will determine whether or not you become a peak performer in every area of your life…

The thing that will determine whether you make massive progress toward the pursuit of your ultimate potential as a human being.

The thing that will determine where you live, where you travel to, where you go to dinner, who your friends are…

The thing that will determine **THE QUALITY OF YOUR LIFE.**

…and let's not forget the people's lives that look to you for the roadmap to how to do life!

That's right.

I'm talking about *mental toughness.*

The biggest problem we have in society today is people getting the wrong advice from people who have no right to be giving it in the first place.

We have self-proclaimed "experts" and "gurus" selling worthless products that don't really solve anyone's problem because they don't get to the core of the problem.

They sell products/books/courses on:

- **How to Have a Happy Marriage**
- **How to Create a Multi-Million-Dollar Online Business**
- **How to Manage Your Money More Effectively**
- **How to Become a Master of Sales**
- **How to Get in Shape in 100 Days**

The list goes on & on & on…

But the dirty little secret is that the vast majority of people who buy these courses don't benefit from them at all.

Why?

Because none of these products are worth **ANYTHING** if the person who buys them lacks the one thing that is essential for success in relationships, business, finances, fitness, and all other aspects of life!

Mental toughness.

And 99.7 percent of the gurus and experts out there don't teach anyone how to be mentally tough, because if they did...hardly anyone would need to buy a course on anything...at least not a course on some general aspect of being happy & successful in life.

Because once you learn what it takes to be mentally tough...

Once you learn how to maximize confidence, self-belief, self-esteem, discipline, determination, perseverance, and grittiness...you can **TRANSFER** those traits to any situation and apply them to any task – in absolutely any area of life.

By learning how to cultivate & master mental toughness – remember, it's the *core* reason anyone is happy & successful – you can teach yourself anything you need to know & learn to how to achieve any goal you set for yourself – from a happy marriage & thriving career to a 7-figure annual income, 8 percent body fat...and beyond!

None of the popular "self-help" or "self-development" courses can provide that for you.

The self-proclaimed "gurus" really have no experience or authority to teach that to you.

And the typical "experts" don't even want to provide that for you.

(Like I said...they wouldn't be able to sell you as much shit.)

So where can you learn how to be mentally tough?

You can learn it from the book you're holding in your hands...
from a program that is unlike **ANYTHING** out there...75HARD.

And who's gonna teach you to be mentally tough?

I am.

Now you're obviously already reading this...so you're already slightly interested and were invested enough to pick this book up.

The concept...

The promise...

The program...

It all intrigues you already, doesn't it?

But because there are so many scammers & scandals out there, I feel a moral obligation to tell you who I am...

...to show you why I'm not like the majority of the idiots out there in the business/entrepreneur & success/motivation space...

...& to explain to you why I know what I'm talking about & can really help you.

So that's what I'm gonna do.

CHAPTER 1
WHO AM I, AND WHY SHOULD YOU LISTEN TO ME?

I'm Andy Frisella.

This is the section where I "establish my street cred."

Let's start when I was a kid, because that's relevant.

Here's the most important thing you need to know about me when I was 7, 8, 10 years old...

When I was a kid, I was fat. And when I say "fat," I don't mean I had a little paunch. I don't mean that I was a little pudgy. I mean I was the fully inflated, Pillsbury-doughboy-kind-of-kid that girls moved their desks to get away from & the popular guys made fun of with names like "Lard Tard," "Chubby Andy," and "Fat Fuck." (Yes, kids do use that kind of language in fourth grade. Stop being naïve and wake up to reality.)

Since I was teased so much, you'd think I would have gotten focused and motivated to lose weight to get the approval and popularity that I desperately wanted. But I was clueless and super lazy. I always had my head in the clouds & my hand in a bag of Doritos.

I will say this about myself: I did have dreams.

Like most people however, I honestly didn't think I had what it took achieve them.

In fact, I didn't even understand the concept of achievement. Like most people, I thought building a cool life was a matter of circumstance or luck or some unforeseen force that somehow through random selection for who knows what reason made certain people successful and others not...some sort of iteration of the concept of predestination in regards to success (a force I refer to as the "Success Fairy").

Even in grade school, most of the kids I knew had some vague sense that they needed to do well in class if they had any hope of not being a total loser when they grew up. But that whole concept was completely lost on me. I really couldn't get myself to care about my homework any more than any kid would care about a local insurance seminar.

The reality is, I didn't care because if I did, I would have had to admit how hard studying was for me. Basic directions confused me. I had to read my assignments over & over & over again & still didn't understand what I read. The teacher would say something & I would need her to repeat it, but I wouldn't raise my hand because I was embarrassed.

It didn't even occur to me that I might have some sort of legit learning disability...that really wasn't a "thing" back then. I just assumed from the irritated and frustrated expressions on people's faces that I was clearly just lazy. Or dumb. Most of the time I felt like I was both.

Things didn't really change as I got older. I did well enough to make it to the next grade level, but not much more.

By the time I reached high school, I had gotten into better shape & was able to do well in sports, but overeating was still a daily struggle, & I was the same old underachieving student—with one exception.

My junior year, I wrote a long research paper on the military aircraft of World War Two. I loved working on that project, because I have always really enjoyed American history, had a huge respect for the armed forces, & have always been fascinated & obsessed with World War Two fighter planes!

So I poured myself into that assignment.

I found out everything I could about the Vought F4U Corsair, the P47 Thunderbolt, the Grumman F6F Hellcat, & my absolute favorite of all time, the North American P-51 Mustang. I was so engrossed in the material that I wrote more & more, until the paper length reached 60 pages!

My teacher was impressed, & I'll be honest with you: it felt good to succeed in an area of life that I thought was a lost cause.

It put some hope in my heart. I started thinking, "well, I've become a decent athlete; so if I can get my grades up, maybe I can play football at one of my two favorite schools: Texas or Notre Dame."

Speaking of Notre Dame...you know that scene in *Rudy* where he's still at Joliet Catholic High School & other students are boarding a bus to visit the University of Notre Dame? He tries to get on the bus himself, but the priest stops him and says, "Rudy, this is not a sight-seeing tour. It's for young men and women considering becoming students at Notre Dame."

Rudy responds, basically saying, "Yeah. That's what I want to do. More than anything!"

That's when they priest pulls him aside and shuts him down.

"Rudy," he says. "This is for the smart kids. You don't do well in school. You'll have to do something else."

(I'm paraphrasing the scene.)

Well, guess what...that same shit happened to me!

I told one of the adults at my high school—I won't say who because I don't want to be a dick—that I really wanted to play football at Texas or Notre Dame.

And this guy, who I really looked up to & respected, said to me, "Both of those schools have academics standards, Andrew. You're not going to be able to cut it." He followed with a line I'll never forget: "Those places are for cream of the crop...not regular guys"

I remember legit thinking: "Fuck you man...one day you're going to regret that statement" and also at the exact same time just feeling like a pissed off loser kid that probably wasn't going to do shit with his life.

You know...nowadays people know me as a guy who is confident, fiery & who has no problem telling people to fuck off when necessary.

But I was just a kid back then. And what he said hurt. It stung....
and it stuck.

Just when I was building some confidence in that area, it sowed some
doubt & discouragement.

So if that's something you have experienced in your life...I get it.

If you feel like you're somehow at a disadvantage because you weren't
born with any sort of mental gifts or superior intelligence either, then
you & I have a lot in common.

That's right. I'm no Einstein & by the way, nobody in my family was or is
an Einstein, either.

Elon Musk wasn't my cousin.

Steve Jobs wasn't my uncle.

I came from a family that wasn't even close to perfect in either
intelligence or in the way we related to each other.

In fact...we were far from it!

My family had (and still has) our share of drama and dysfunction.
If I actually told you all the specifics, you'd think it was like something
you'd see on that crazy old talk show, Jerry Springer.

I promise, you wouldn't even believe me even if I told you.

I don't tell you that to make you feel sorry for me.

And I don't tell you that to rip on my relatives.

The fact is, I believe 100 percent that you can speak the truth about
what's fucked up in your family & still love being part of it. You can
acknowledge that people are messed up & still love & appreciate them.

I tell you that about my family because I'm guessing that many of you
can relate.

Your family tree is probably full of deadbeat dads, crackhead uncles &

juvenile delinquent cousins…

You share DNA with scammers, sluts, blue collar buffoons, & white-collar criminals.

The conversations you've had with relatives could be part of a reality show script.

The things you've seen in your family life could be recorded and go viral in a couple minutes.

That's why I want to tell you…I get it!

I was & am in the same boat as you might be.

I don't have royal blood in my veins.

So I am very, very confident that there's nothing you faced growing up that I didn't.

But…

I did have one, huge, incredible go-to resource in my family that maybe you didn't.

A great dad.

A dad who taught me life-changing lessons.

A dad who knew that he needed to drill hard truths into my head over & over & over again until they finally "took."

CHAPTER 2
KILL! KILL! KILL!

I am genuinely sorry for you if your dad is a loser & you don't want to be anything like him.

Me?

My dad has always been my ultimate rock and role model.

Like me ... he wasn't some gifted genius.

He wasn't Jesus either...he did a lot wrong...but he always made sure to point out his own mistakes to my brother Sal & I to try and help us avoid them. That's the part I always will respect most about my Dad. He owned his own shit. Always.

He was rarely the smartest person in the room, but he preferred it that way so he could improve at every opportunity.

What he lacked in "smarts" he made up for in determination & work ethic (today at 70+ years old...nobody can physically or mentally outwork him).

In a way, my dad's childhood is like a country music song. He was born in 1945 and grew up poor, living in a ramshackle house built on a gravel road in rural Missouri.

Today if you drive around the place my dad grew up, you can still find people who are pretty poor. But somehow they can still afford to pay for big screen TVs and Satellite dishes.

What the fuck, right?

My dad's experience being poor was pretty different.

His father was an ox. He'd get up early to go to work and stay late. There wasn't a lazy bone in his body. Because of this, the family always had the basic necessities of life...

A house over their head.

Clothes to wear.

Food to eat.

The thing is...my dad was one of twelve—that's right, *twelve*—kids. And since both of his parents weren't just hard-working, but also frugal and no-nonsense kind of people, my dad rarely wore clothes that hadn't previously been worn by an older brother.

His mom also refused to provide a limitless supply of food for her army of a family.

"We had to rush to the dinner table," he once told me. "If you didn't get there right away, there was a good chance you weren't going to get anything to eat!"

Bottom line...my dad's parents were the definition of "old school." If something broke, they didn't buy a replacement. They fixed it. Or they got creative and jerry-rigged a solution to the problem.

Before you start feeling sorry for my dad, you need to know that his circumstances growing up produced a mentally that drove his success.

That mentality is this: success in life requires tenacity. You do everything you have to do in life to make things **WORK.**

So growing up in his family...newspapers became napkins.

Old wood from broken furniture became material to build **NEW** furniture.

Literally...my dad was taught that you should never, ever make excuses in life.

You just find a way.

Guess what? The lesson took.

As he got older...he made things work!

He made things happen!

He eventually pulled himself out of poverty by becoming a businessman.

He worked his ass off, starting an electrical company in St. Louis & growing it until it had hundreds of employees & generated millions of dollars in revenue.

Millions of dollars, I might add...that my dad barely ever spent and **THANKFULLY** never gave even a dime of to me.

For my dad, that would have been ruining his son. That would have been depriving me of the lessons that he learned himself about what it takes to succeed in life.

So instead of giving me and my brother Sal money, he gave us hell!

He pushed us.

He drove us.

He'd always have us repeat what he called "The Frisella Family Battle Cry."

I'm talking about three words we heard over & over again growing up:

"KILL! KILL! KILL!"

Those three words pretty much sum up my dad's approach to parenting. And life.

One of my earliest memories is of my dad giving Sal and me each a pair of boxing gloves and making us box. We were three and four years old!

As we got older, we played all sorts of sports. Football, baseball, wrestling, lacrosse, hockey—you name it. And my dad didn't want us to just participate in sporting events.

He wanted us to dominate them!

As we were driving to a football game or soccer game or whatever, my dad would say, "Now, boys, listen up! When you get in there you've got to be aggressive. You've got to go in the corner and you've got to get that fucking puck out!"

He'd always say "puck." Even if we weren't playing hockey. "Dad," we'd say. "This is soccer." "I don't care what it is!" he'd say. "You just go in there and get it!" "What are you going to do today?" he'd ask, as serious as if he was commanding troops in battle. "Kill!" we'd yell in our squeaky, pre-pubescent voices, a juxtaposition sounding like a couple of murderous thugs from a boy choir. Straight out of *Lord of the Flies*.

It was also understood that if, during a game, we ran over another kid or we scored a goal, we got a toy. We'd get to go to K-Mart or Wal-Mart afterward and pick out a good one. Not some Cracker Jack prize or trinket from a bubble gum machine. A legit toy—like a G.I. Joe action figure or a Transformer or something like that.

"What are you going to do?" my dad would ask a second time.

"Kill! Kill! Kill!"

Some people get all offended by that story because they don't understand the point my dad was trying to make.

It was never about hurting people.

It was never about getting toys.

It wasn't even about sports.

My dad wanted to teach us to be aggressive. He wanted us to be competitive, because he knew that what Rocky Balboa said was true:

"The world ain't all sunshine and rainbows. It's a very mean and nasty place, and I don't care how tough you are, it will beat you to your knees and keep you there permanently, if you let it. You, me or nobody, is gonna hit as hard as life. But it ain't about how hard you hit. It's about how hard you can get hit, and keep moving forward, how much you can take, and keep moving forward. That's how winning is done."

My dad knew that life is hard, and that in order to succeed in anything, you have to develop a mindset and personal conduct that is serious as blood and tough as mother fucking nails. He knew that success requires a killer competitive attitude and an unparalleled will to win.

My dad was..and is...a *realist* about life. As am I.

And people who are *realists* understand that life...I'm talking about our whole human existence and experience...is set up for *competition*.

Think about it...

You look at a video game made for a two-year-old: It keeps score. Life on planet Earth is not kindergarten. It's kill or be killed. The world is not a playground. It's a battleground. It's not syrup and sweetness. It's survival of the fittest. In the real world, nobody cares about your feelings, your self-esteem, or your need for significance.

The real world deals in facts, not feelings, and what matters is action, execution, and results. The reality is, history forgets whiners, but remembers winners.

Bottom line: <u>The nature of real life demands that we see the pursuit of happiness and success and greatness as a competition—and only tough-minded, hard-working, straight-shooting people win that competition.</u>

The only people who win...and win BIG at life...are people with <u>MENTAL TOUGHNESS.</u>

That's the message he was trying to drive into my head every single time we shouted out The Frisella Family Battle Cry:

Kill! Kill! Kill!

BE AGGRESSIVE.

BE FEROCIOUS.

GO HARD AFTER WHAT YOU WANT AND NEVER GIVE UP.

In a phrase: **MASTER MENTAL TOUGHNESS.**

That's what my dad was trying to teach me.

THAT WAS HIS POINT.

I got his point. And it's made all the difference for me.

CHAPTER 3

THE BACKSTORY OF MY BUSINESS SUCCESS

In 1999, along with my best friend Chris, I started a business with nothing. Absolutely nothing.

No money. Not a single clue.

At just 19 years old, Chris and I decided we were going to open a vitamin & supplement retail store. We knew a guy who was "crushing it" and we thought we could do the same.

Truth be told, our first idea was to open a tanning salon. But, we only had $12,000 between us (that we earned from painting the stripes on parking lots in the summer) and a single tanning bed was around 30k so we quickly realized that wasn't an option.

So we finally decided on supplements.

We both worked out. We knew a guy who was doing well at it. So we thought we could do it too.

We needed a location so we went to nearly every vacant retail spot in Springfield Missouri trying to rent a space.

Nobody would rent to us. 99% of the time we couldn't even get a phone call in return.

We were 19, had no credit, had no financial backing...I wouldn't have rented to us, either.

We searched high and low and came across a location that was in an old bridal store. It was far from ideal. It was old, ratty and smelled like mothballs & dust.

However, that landlord—a really nice guy named Mark—agreed to rent to us.

But there was a catch.

He wanted a year's rent up front. Rent was $1,000 a month.

As I mentioned, we only had $12,000 between us. So we did what we had to do. We paid the man.

Every dime we had.

To build out the store, make it presentable, & stock it, we figured we could get some credit cards.

We went around campus and filled out every credit card application we could. Back then these credit card companies would set up tables and give out T-shirts to incentivize kids to sign up for their cards....and they were **EVERYWHERE** on campus. So we filled them **ALL** out.

And with a bunch of $600 max limit credit cards we started a company.

We bought supplies at Home Depot and with the help of some family & friends we built our counter & shelves out of 2x4s, plywood and corrugated roofing tin. (It was quality craftsmanship because our first retail store on South Campbell in Springfield Mo still uses this counter 20+ years later).

We painted the store ourselves.

I had a high school friend, Tom Young, who was an amazing artist (now a successful architect), draw us a logo. He charged us $50. (It took me 3 years to be able to pay him)

We literally knew **NOTHING** about supplements or running a business...
but like most 19-year old entrepreneurs we wanted to make millions...
we **EXPECTED** to make millions.

So like I do with so many things...I ran with all my energy, enthusiasm
and will to win, and like a bull in a china shop and I made a mess...
a big one.

I remember opening on our first day of business in 1999 thinking we were
going to be big ballers.

We were going to be millionaires by the age of 20 and my entire life was
going to be popping bottles with models and driving Lambos.

I knew it was our destiny.

That first day was something legends are made of...just not the kind of
legend I expected at the time.

We saw exactly **ONE** customer.

One. Not a few. Not our families. Not our friends. **ONE FUCKING
PERSON** walked into Supplement Superstores on our first day
in business.

His name was Nick Vespa.

He bought a $7 bottle of "fat burners"...and I'm 100% sure he did so
because he felt sorry for us...and it was the cheapest product we sold in
the store.

In fact, I know it, because years later he told me that was
the case.

The second day, we saw zero customers.

The third day, we saw one customer who spent $23.
By this time, reality was sinking in.

I knew we had made a mistake (or so I thought).

I knew we were in over our heads...but at this point what else could
we do?

We had no money.

We had no place to live.

We were sleeping on and off on a used mattress in the back of the store.

We got it from a Salvation Army Store that our store shared occupancy within the same retail shopping center.

This mattress had a stain that I believe was urine on it, and I can remember trying not to ever lay my head on the urine stain believing the urine would somehow run up my drool and into my mouth if I slept on it.

We were definitely not living in the lap of luxury. Far from it.

We had zero options.

We had to stick it out.

It was slow.

Very slow.

Many days we saw one or two people.

A busy day was 4 people.

It took us 8 months to have a day over $200.

Chris & I both had to work multiple other jobs to even keep the store operational.

During the first year 3 years of business, we made ZERO dollars.

During years 3-10, I never made more than $695 per month.

So for many years, I had to work other jobs AND run my business AND go to college (because it's what I was "supposed" to do).

I had to do anything & everything I could to keep my store open and running.

And I'm telling you...I made every mistake possible.

And sometimes those mistakes were **BAD** ones.

But I've always been stubborn (my Dad called me "rock head." Dad...
if your reading this you need better nick names...your shit talk game is
weak) & I always refused to quit at anything I did, no matter how much it
confused or frustrated me, until **I FIGURED IT OUT.**

Hey...it took me 18+ years, but eventually **I DID** figure it out.

We figured out how to be so mentally tough that – no matter what, come
hell or high water – I wasn't going to give up.

I was going to power through.

I was going to become who I wanted to become & do what I said I was
going to do.

And guess what?

That's exactly what happened.

I figured out how to take a cash-strapped startup with no budget and
turn it into a 9-figure business that was booming.

Today, in addition to serving as CEO of one of the world's leading
nutritional supplement companies, 1st Phorm International, I founded
and run (at the time of this writing) six other businesses that collectively
generate mid-nine figures in annual revenue.

At times, I have to pinch myself because it seems like a dream. If I'm
honest, there were times I wondered if my dream was ever really going to
come true.

Especially since about 3-4 years into my entrepreneurial journey, I
experienced a nightmare that didn't just threaten my business...

It threatened my life!

CHAPTER 4
STABBED IN SPRINGFIELD

In June of 2004, on a hot night in Springfield, Missouri, I was lying face down on the pavement, my face and body gushing blood.

Two of my friends & I had been minding our business, walking back from a club, when this guy started spewing racial slurs at the female friend from his car. I confronted him, we had words, and I started to walk away.

When I turned my back on him, he attacked me.

I wasn't expecting it & when a guy with a knife attacks you by surprise, trust me...he can do serious damage before you even know what's happening.

He stabbed me multiple times, the blade ripping into my face.
I still remember the warm sticky rush of blood gushing out of my face and mouth and down my chest.

This dude...who, by the way, at the time of this incident had pending charges for beating a kid with a baseball bat...probably would have finished me off if it wasn't for my good friend, Scott.

Scott pulled the guy off me & then started going after this guy, but the guy ran off.

He ran away & left me for dead!

The last thing I remember before blacking out was the EMT in the ambulance yelling that they couldn't stop the bleeding.

I was 100% convinced I was going to **DIE.**

Obviously, I was wrong. I lived—but I ended up receiving 160 stitches in my face alone. If you know me or have ever seen a photo of me, you know that the scars remain to this day. They have faded a lot, but they are there—a jagged line running from my nose across my right cheek to my ear.

And they aren't little.

They aren't inconspicuous.

The worst one, and first one, runs along my jawline from one side of my neck to the other. This is where he tried to slice my throat from behind.

It's mostly covered by my beard these days.

Even with the beard, you know they are there.

Every morning, I wake up and see the evidence of that night.

I'm constantly, every single day, reminded of that night. I can still run my finger along my scars and remember— like it was yesterday—how bad it hurt.

But you know what?

The physical trauma was the easiest thing to handle.

Once they got me to the hospital, the doctors gave me some drugs to help ease my pain. Plus, the human body is amazingly resilient. It has incredible powers of healing, and when its survival is threatened, it finds ways to cope.

Actually, when it came to coping, my body did a better job than I did.

During my recovery, my face got all swollen and bloated. I looked ridiculous—like Sloth from The Goonies or something. (Okay, maybe not that bad. But I definitely looked weird, and I knew people would notice.)

For a while, I was really embarrassed. In fact, for almost two years, I was very sensitive and stressed out about the whole thing.

Sometimes I didn't even go outside for **WEEKS ON END** other than to go to get basic supplies for living.

I was **TERRIFIED** of being around other people.

I remember going to Bass Pro Shop to look at shotguns. My face still looked pretty bad and the sales guy there was an asshole. He acted like he didn't see me, and after I had to go out of my way to get his attention, he acted disgusted that he had to look at my face.

I was **PISSED.**

But I also felt **REJECTED.**

When I went out in public, I noticed more and more that people wouldn't talk to me; or when they did **THEY WOULDN'T LOOK ME IN THE FACE.**

They'd look at their **FUCKING FEET.**

I felt like I was going through this process of social rejection.

I wasn't prepared for it.

And nobody really told me to expect it.

I went from being a normal dude to being **SOMEBODY PEOPLE DIDN'T TALK TO.**

This wouldn't be a huge deal except I had just started a business. I was in retail. I would talk to customers every day. It kind of fucked up my plan.

Some people were cool and asked, "Man, what happened?" in a nice way, but a lot of people were extremely rude and insensitive.

They'd laugh and say, "Dude, what the **FUCK** happened to your face?"

It **HURT.**

It **BEAT ME UP.**

Especially because I couldn't retaliate or defend myself.

Snapping back at someone for insulting your face isn't a great way to get repeat customers.

One time I had a guy come in the store. I'd never seen him before.

He walked directly to the counter and said to me: **"DUDE WHAT THE FUCK HAPPENED TO YOU"** loudly.

It fucking pissed me off so bad.

I held it in.

I lied and told the guy I had been in a car accident. I didn't want to really talk to this guy at all.

He then proceeded to walk over to this big wall of bars we had.
Where we had literally 30 different kinds of bars and goes:
"Yo...how much are theses bars?"

I replied "Well, as I'm sure you can see we have 30 different kinds of bars" in an admittedly smart ass tone.

The guy detected my annoyance and looked at me with a smart ass look and says: "Is that how you talk to all the customers" ...

I said "No sir, just the asshole ones".

So you can see how this was a problem for my business.

Either take everyone's bullshit or be broke.

Those were my options.

When you are in kindergarten they tell you, "It's who you are on the inside that matters," and that's probably true.

But let's face it: right or wrong, people judge you by your face. And I knew that. So I was worried that my scars would **RUIN MY LIFE.**

When I worked out at the gym, bought food at the grocery store, or hung out at a bar, were people going to stare at me?

Could I have a conversation with someone without them being distracted by my face?

Would the douchebags of the world crack jokes behind my back?

(In hindsight I can tell you the answers are: Yes, Rarely & Yes respectively)

I went through a lot of tough mental **SHIT.**

I felt **SORRY** for myself.

I thought my life was **OVER.**

I thought, "No girl is ever going to want to date me. I look like a **FUCKING MONSTER.**" And here's what I think happened: it became a self-fulfilling prophecy.

I isolated myself because I was afraid of rejection.

I started drinking real hard.

I smoked weed constantly to escape the emotional pain.

I stopped focusing on my goals.

Bottom line: I got depressed. Really depressed. Really **REALLY** depressed.

And then, I met the most unlikely hero in the most unlikely place.

A person who changed **EVERYTHING.**

CHAPTER 5

PROFOUND MOMENT AT PRICE CUTTER

I was pushing a cart through a Price Cutter, shopping for some groceries—probably beer. I came to the end of an aisle and accidentally bumped somebody else's cart as they were turning around the corner.

I started to say, "I'm sorry," still looking into my cart. But then I looked up. And here's the reality: I couldn't really tell at first whether the person in front of me was a man or a woman—because his or her face was so badly burned.

And guess what?

I looked away. I did the same shit that people had done to me.

But this lady—that's what she was—didn't miss a beat.

"Hey!" she said.

"WHAT THE FUCK HAPPENED TO YOUR FACE?"

I looked back up at her face and saw a big grin. We both burst into laughter. Obviously, we both understood that people do say and think that kind of shit. We ended up having a conversation for ten minutes.

That single conversation changed my whole life.

This lady had been in a plane crash that killed five people. Somehow, she was the only one who survived, though she had been burned from head to toe. We talked about what she went through and how she had learned to overcome it, and how she lived with gratitude. I talked about what I had gone through.

It put things in **PERSPECTIVE.**

And when I walked out of Price Cutter, I felt healed. Cured.

INSTANTLY.

CHAPTER 6

TURNING SCARS INTO STRENGTHS

After meeting that lady, I said: "**FUCK IT!** I'm not going to drown in self-pity anymore. I'm not going to complain. I'm done being depressed."

I decided to stop being an ass who bitched about his scars. Instead, I chose to be a man who embraced his scars as an asset. I chose to believe that somehow, some way, getting stabbed and having scars on my face was—wait for it—a good thing.

No. **A GREAT THING.**

You're probably thinking, "Are you kidding me, Andy?"

No. I'm dead serious. And it turns out, I was right.

IF YOU ARE TRYING to build a successful business, the last thing you want is for people to forget who you are.

If they remember you, they will remember your business.

If they remember your business, there's a better chance they'll become customers.

For that reason, when entrepreneurs or business people are networking, they do what they can to be memorable. They come up with a catchy slogan, compelling pitch, or creative business card to stand out from the crowd.

Guess what I learned?

Turns out that having a sliced-up face is great for carving a niche in people's minds.

As my partner Chris and I were working on our supplements business, I started noticing something pretty cool: my scars were giving us a competitive edge. How? They helped people remember me—and, by extension, our business.

Like any good entrepreneur, I tried to spread the word about our business by being outgoing, friendly, articulate, and enthusiastic to everyone I met. But the truth is, a lot of people in business are outgoing, friendly, articulate, and enthusiastic. Those qualities alone won't necessarily distinguish you from the pack.

But scars from stab wounds to the face? That's unique.

And I discovered that once people met me, they remembered me and what I did for a living...even if they didn't remember my name:

"Oh, yeah, that dude with the scars," they'd say. "He runs that supplement store."

Or, "That's the guy who got stabbed in the face. Dude helps people get ripped."

In many cases, people actually asked me how I got the scars, so I'd tell them the story. And you know what? They NEVER forgot.

We sometimes forget facts and statistics, but STORIES always stay with us. They are really easy to remember if they involve something traumatic or graphic—like getting stabbed in the face. Because of my scars—and my story—I became unique in the minds of the people I met. (Hopefully, my sparkling personality had something to do with it, too.)

Crazy as it sounds, what had happened to me gave me an advantage. **A BIG ONE.**

Bottom line: Getting stabbed in the face was great for business.

Did you read that right?

Read it again carefully.

And think about that.

I mean, really think about it.

Is that the attitude the average person would take?

No.

But, through my experience of powering through business struggles, the brutal trauma & aftermath of getting stabbed, I've developed bullet-proof mental toughness.

And I've told you the back story of my business & near-death experience to drive home a point:

The mental toughness I've had to develop professionally & personally has paid dividends. HUGE dividends.

It's paid off in business.

It's paid off in life.

CHAPTER 7
RISE OF THE MFCEO

Because of everything that I'd experienced and learned in my life, in 2015 I started seriously thinking about writing a book to share my experience and knowledge.

I knew I had something good to share with people.

I knew I could help them...not just build a business, but build the mindset that it would take to succeed at anything in life.

But the reality is, what motivated me the most was anger.

I saw how so many so-called "experts" and "gurus" on the internet were hosting podcasts & selling courses on "how to sell like a champ" & "how to build an 8-figure business." The problem was the only thing they ever sold was an internet course & the only thing they "built" was an online business dedicated to manipulating people!

I knew that I knew how to sell & I knew that I understood how to build a **REAL** business, from the ground up.

I learned in **REAL LIFE** what it took to create a winning culture, to attract & cultivate loyal customers, & to scale a business from one retail store to a full-out, vertically integrated multi-million-dollar empire.

I understood what it really took to be a successful entrepreneur & it pissed me off to no end that good people who wanted to see their entrepreneurial dreams become reality were getting lied to and ripped off!

Well, just about the time I was thinking through what I wanted to say in my book, a local St. Louis magazine sent a guy out to my office to write an article about me and the success of my businesses.

He and I met and hit it off pretty good; mostly because we started out by talking about how much both of us loved our dogs. The interview went great & he ended writing an article that I really liked. When he stopped back by our office to drop off copies of the magazine, he said to me, "hey man, I was going over my notes. You have some seriously great experience and insights. Have you ever considered writing a book?"

Of course, I told him "yes," & that I was a pretty good writer myself and was thinking about writing a book, but that I was just crazy busy.

"Well," he said. "The world needs what you have to offer. Why don't you let me help you get the book going?"

I thought that was a great idea; so we started meeting regularly.

We would pick a topic—like sales or customer service or the mental challenges of entrepreneurship—& he would interview me. He'd ask me all sorts of questions, getting me to unpack all of my thoughts on a particular topic, & most of the time, I'd really get into what I was talking about & start really spitting out some cool stuff.

Well, in order to have those sessions transcribed into notes for the book, I would have one of the guys on my company's creative team record the sessions in both video & audio.

On a whim, I decided to post some of the clips from the interviews on social media—Instagram and Facebook. The video clips would show me talking about some aspect of business or success. They weren't long. At the time 15 seconds max.

But guess what?

When people saw them, they went crazy!

All of a sudden, I started getting emails & text messages & DMs asking saying, "this shit is incredible!" and asking me, "where can I listen to your podcast?"

And honest to God, my first thought was, "podcast? I don't have a fucking podcast! I'm writing books...you know, real shit, not that weird nerd podcast shit"

I was completely ignorant to the whole podcast world & thought that was just something that computer nerds were into.

I realized very quickly how wrong I was.

I also realized that...in many ways, more than a book...a podcast was the perfect platform to teach people what I've learned about business & life in a very engaging, dynamic way—through a conversation.

So I said, "That's it. That's what I'm going to do! I'm going start a podcast!"

I asked that writer, Vaughn Kohler, to become the co-host and my producer to start running the audio & video for the podcast.

I decided to name it The MFCEO Project.

Why?

Well, long story short...

My favorite online video ever is a K-Swiss commercial on YouTube where Kenny Powers, the legendary character from East Bound & Down series becomes the MFCEO of K-Swiss. It's hilarious. Go YouTube it.

I used to play this video in our office and walk around saying the jokes he said in the videos. So much so that one of our creative designers, Terri Spencer, had a shirt made that said "MFCEO" on it.

Because I am The Mother Fucking CEO! ...in real life. You watch that commercial...that's me in real life. I'm not this serious, mad, angry dude...I'm a jokester, a clown, and someone who loves to make people laugh in unconventional ways by just being who I am...while still kicking all kinds of ass.

That character is as close to what I have seen to what I'm actually like in day-to-day and the name stuck.

And I wanted to teach other people to be The MFCEO of their own lives.

To scale their businesses to 7, 8 & 9-figures.

To crush their goals.

Above all...to absolutely master the qualities it takes to be successful, not just in business, but in all of life.

The qualities I mentioned earlier...discipline, confidence, grit, determination, fortitude, perseverance...

...all those skills that add up to the one thing that is more invaluable than anything else: mental toughness!

You know what?

As of the writing of this book, we've released more than 300 episodes & it's been a wild ride!

We've covered every possible topic from productivity & peak performance to being able to focus & live with a constant sense of urgency.

We've had great guests on the show like Jocko Willink, Tim Grover, Gary Vaynerchuk, The Diesel Brothers, Sean Whalen, James Lawrence, Tyron Woodly, Ben Newman, Lewis Howes and my good friend and co-founder of The Arete Syndicate: Ed Mylett.

Right out of the gate, tons of people started downloading our episodes.

Today we get millions of listeners every month & we consistently rank #1 out of all the business and success podcasts **IN THE WORLD.**

And that doesn't even begin to cover everything!

CHAPTER 8
FROM PODCASTING TO PLATFORM SPEAKER AND BEYOND

The MFCEO Project podcast has led to other really cool experiences and opportunities.

I've become one of the highest paid keynote speakers in the world. I've even written a best-selling series of children's books called Otis & Charley's Hardworking Tails that promote entrepreneurial values and the success mindset, when it matters most, in the beginning.

Along with Ed Mylett, I founded an elite society of entrepreneurs called The Arete Syndicate. It's a group that is committed to scaling their businesses to 9-figures, crushing their personal and professional goals, and being a force for good in the world.

There's so many scammers and con arts in the world of business. In my mind, The Arete Syndicate is going to fix that. It's going to be a movement that transforms entrepreneurship & the whole world...for the good! (You can learn more about it at aretesyndicate.com, by the way.)

Over the last couple years, I've been recognized as one of the world's leading authorities on customer retention and loyalty and company culture, as well as the marketing techniques it takes to build both brick-and-mortar and online direct-to-consumer retail businesses from the ground up.

I was identified as Entrepreneur of the Year in 2016 and have been featured in Forbes (yes, a little fat kid who grew up on a gravel road in Missouri was featured in Forbes...a few times actually), INC, and Entrepreneur Magazine as well as many other honorable publications.

So yes...I've done a few things.

I've experienced my share of what other people might call "success."

I've got the recognition.

I enjoy the perks, lifestyle and "the toys."

Let's talk about that for a second.

Now listen...It's important you understand that 75Hard is not a "get rich program"...it's not really even focused on money at all... but there is a place for motivating ourselves with material goals & the reality is that <u>one</u> indication that we have become mentally tough is our ability to create wealth.

So let's talk about material things for just a second.

Let's talk about cars & mansions & making a lot of money.

CHAPTER 9
CARS, CRIBS, AND THE REALLY COOL SHIT

I've always been a 'car guy', so it's been a thrill for me to indulge that passion as I've become financially successful.

Ferraris. Aston Martins. Rolls Royces. Porsches. Ford GTs. All sorts of muscle cars.

(I'm a sucker for late 60's Muscle.)

Really, whatever car I want, but as much as I love cars, what really thrills me these days, is my home!

I live on a property that used to belong to *Ulysses S. Grant.*

Do you know who that is?

If you're an American, you should probably recognize the name; he was the general who led Union forces during the Civil War. He commanded the side that *won.* After the war, he was elected the 18th president of the United States, and around that time, he bought some land outside St. Louis, Missouri and built an impressive estate on the land which is known today as Grant's Farm.

What people *don't* realize, is that he also owned a plot of land "down the street" (about 10 min down the road in a car, but a full day's journey by horse and carriage) that was his "hunting property".

Eventually, an amazing house was built on that land. I mean a Southern colonial style fucking mansion of a house, with Roman columns, and the kind of balcony you'd see in the famous movie *Gone with the Wind...*only GRANDER.

The first time I saw that house, I was blown away.

It was my dream home, and I knew I would live there someday!
I was 1000 percent confident of that fact! Even though, at the time, I didn't have enough money to pay for the front door, let alone the whole house!

But I knew.

In October of 2018, I bought that house, and after an extensive renovation I moved into it in May of 2019.

The amazing mansion, built on the land once owned by the general who won the Civil War and the 18th president of the United States, *is now mine.*

I live there with my wife and three bulldogs (Otis, Charley & Ellie). Oh, and by the way; I also have a 200-acre farm 25 minutes away that would give Churchill Downs a run for its money.

Don't get me wrong; I'm not bragging.

I'm not trying to be "Tommy Topper." (You know who Tommy Topper is. He's the dude who annoys the shit out of you at parties or meetings. Who is always trying to "top" anything you say. You know Tommy, we all have one in our life)

That ain't me. I'm making an important point.

How did I get all that material shit?

MENTAL TOUGHNESS.

More importantly than the material, though, how did I gain the freedom to do whatever I want, whenever I want, and answer to absolutely nobody?

MENTAL TOUGHNESS.

Here's what you really need to understand; as amazing as it is to experience and enjoy all the cool things that come with developing mental toughness in your own life, I've discovered that it's not near as cool as helping **OTHER PEOPLE** develop mental toughness so that they can experience and enjoy the same things, too!

In other words - and I believe 100 percent that you'll learn this, if you haven't already:

THERE'S NOTHING BETTER THAN HELPING PEOPLE.

Me, personally, I love teaching men and women the skills they need to succeed.

I love teaching them how, and pushing them to pursue the fulfillment of their own true potential.

Seeing people take what I give them, and build their ultimate life, is an amazing experience. Seeing one of my employees buy a new house or car or hit some other goal because of the skills I taught them is what really gets me going.

Making a real impact, and seeing it happen before your eyes; *that's what I love.*

So read this next paragraph very carefully:

I firmly believe that no matter who you are; man or woman; how intelligent you are; how talented you are; no matter what skills you lack; how good looking or not you happen to be; no matter how meek or modest, or loud and boisterous; you **CAN** develop **MENTAL TOUGHNESS** and become extremely successful in business and life.

You can have the discipline!

You can have the determination!

You can create the confidence!

You can develop the grit & fortitude & self-belief.

I did it! You can too!

And you can enjoy all the results that come with developing mental toughness!

The material stuff.

The "meaningful" stuff.

The freedom to become who you are meant to be.

The freedom to live however **YOU** want.

The choice is yours.

So all of that brings me to this point; If you want to 'have it all' in life, you really do have to have the things I just mentioned:

You have to have confidence.

You have to have self-belief.

You have to have discipline.

You have to have determination.

You have to perseverance.

You have to have tenacity.

You have to have grit.

The bottom line is that you need what all of those things combine together to form.

You must have what all of those individual traits add up to:

MENTAL TOUGHNESS.

If you possess mental toughness, possess it in ever-increasing measures:

You will win.

Win **BIG.**

And win at **EVERYTHING.**

If you're willing to learn. I can teach you.

Hell, **I WANT** to teach you!

I want to teach you about mental toughness, and help you master it!
I want to teach you everything I can about the most important thing you can possess for success and happiness!

Wait…*happiness* too? Not just success?

That's right. This program is all about achieving success and happiness. That's why I created 75HARD.

Let me tell you how.

CHAPTER 10

TWENTY YEARS AND IT FINALLY "CLICKED": HOW 75HARD CAME INTO EXISTENCE

Here's what you need to understand; I've been learning everything I could about mental toughness for the last 20 years.

I've read books.

I've watched videos.

I've listened to audio programs.

I've consulted experts.

I've gained my own lessons in the crucible of real life.

BUT, I'm releasing this program to the public **NOW** because of a breakthrough I had recently; an ah-ha moment that provided the spark for finally putting it all together!

On one of The MFCEO Project podcast episodes in early 2019, my guest was James Lawrence, aka The Iron Cowboy. He's the dude who completed *50 Iron Mans in 50 days in 50 different states.*

It was an unbelievable accomplishment. Something I don't think will ever be done again. James is hands down one of the most mentally tough dudes I have ever met, if not *the* toughest.

At one point during our conversation, he was talking about owning the mental conversation with yourself:

"To be successful at the highest levels, you have to do stuff you don't like. It's part of the formula. We're moving forward or we're moving backwards, and if you're not uncomfortable, you're moving backwards."

Well, I've always known that was the key to happiness and success, but to hear someone else say it like that? Someone who has done something to the extreme that he has done? It made something click in my brain, and it clicked instantly. The whole puzzle that I'd been thinking about for the last 20 years - about how to create mental toughness - it just came to me in that moment.

In the podcast, I actually stopped him and I said, "Whoa, you said something powerful. You said something that is key to cultivating mental toughness."

What did James say? He said this:

"The number one key to cultivating mental toughness is to intentionally put yourself in places that are uncomfortable."

And as I thought about the last twenty years, I realized that was exactly what I had done. It was what I had done for years, without really knowing what I was doing or understanding why I did it.

I had intentionally put myself in uncomfortable situations - I had intentionally chosen to do **HARD THINGS** - and that's how I had developed the skills of confidence & self-discipline & grit & all that.

That's how I have created **MENTAL TOUGHNESS.**

As I was thinking about all of this, I made another connection in my head; I had another life-changing realization. **Ah-ha moment #2!**

I realized that becoming mentally tough was the single greatest factor in my own HAPPINESS. Now, you might be thinking; "Andy, what the fuck are you talking about? Doing hard things & creating mental toughness makes you happy?"

Yes! That is 100 percent true! That is what I am saying, and if you understand that, and start embracing that, you and your life will never be the same!

So pay attention to what you're about to read, because this is huge:

HARD = HAPPY.

If you asked most people if they want to do hard things, they'd say "no way!"

So if you told someone, "picture happiness," the vast majority of people would absolutely not picture themselves working their asses off! Instead, they would picture themselves sitting on the beach, drinking a beer, kicking back and relaxing. Why? Because that's the picture of happiness you have been **SOLD** your entire life.

Retirement!

Easy Street!

Beaches!

Sand!

Stupid looking umbrella drinks!

You didn't come up with that shit on your own!

Look around and pay attention and you'll see very quickly that the things people say make them happy really don't at all. And if you look closer, you'll see that the marketing never aligns with the reality. The truth of the matter is, if you're honest with yourself, the moments you feel best about yourself *are right after you just did something really fucking hard:*

You trained for a marathon and, in spite of all your fear and self-doubt, you finished it.

You finally decided to confront the intimidating co-worker who treats you like shit, and you defended yourself!

You invested hours and hours into a presentation for a major client - an account no one thought you were going to get - and you closed the deal!

You finally decided to quit drinking after years and years of struggling with alcoholism, and after going to 90 straight days of AA and working the program every day after that, you achieved your first year of sobriety!

You competed in an Iron Man.

You severed ties with a person you loved, but who is extremely toxic.

You finally earned your pilot's license.

You won a fitness competition.

The list is endless, but what is fact is that every time you did something **HARD** - even though you struggled, even though it was humiliating at times; even though you failed again & again before you started making real progress; eventually, when you achieved success; when you **COMPLETED** that incredibly difficult task, you felt...

AMAZING!

Your level of happiness was off the charts, because you hadn't just done something hard; you had become someone far better.

That's what happens when you do hard things; your level of happiness is tied in direct proportion to how much discipline you are currently exercising.

ALL THE PIECES FELL INTO PLACE

When I had these two great realizations all the pieces fell into place. I realized the connection between doing hard things & developing mental toughness, and when I went home that night I was fired up!

I'd figured out what I needed to do!

I needed to come up with a program that created mental toughness, and the guiding principle of that program, was going to be getting people to intentionally put themselves in places that are uncomfortable!

Not only that, but I needed to get them to do that long enough that it would become a part of who they were! So much so that it would radically transform their lives, and produce the kind of satisfaction with themselves, and happiness with their lives, that they had never experienced before!

In other words; I had to get people to do things that are hard. The things that I have learned that can consistently develop, and fine tune the skill of mental toughness, day in and day out:

On purpose.

Every day.

For a long fucking time.

But how long was long enough?

Well, at that time, I had $250,000 bet going on with the other members of The Arete Syndicate, which is an elite group of overachieving entrepreneurs that I founded with Ed Mylett. I made this pledge that I would get down to 10 percent body fat or less by our next meeting, which was May 18, 2019. That day happened to be 75 days from the day I had my epiphany about mental toughness.

So I thought; "okay, I'm locking in for the next 75 days. I know I'm committed to my goal, and mentally tough enough to accomplish it, and since I'm taking the next 75 days to lock in on my goals, and since 75 is a pretty long period of time, I'll ask people to join me!

"I'll ask them to do hard things to develop mental toughness, every day, for the next 75 days!"

That's why I call it 75Hard.

I revealed the program on my podcast and on social media, and literally thousands upon thousands of people pledged to do it!

I invited them to join me.

Now I'm inviting **you.**

I guarantee it will teach you how to cultivate mental toughness.

I guarantee that by the end of the 75 days, you will not be the same person; your life will be transformed!

I guarantee that if you do everything you are supposed to do, you're going to experience a kind of happiness that is only experienced by an elite minority of people on the Earth; the people who have paid the price to win the prize of mental toughness!

Before we even get into the nitty-gritty, I'm going to zero in on the epic battle; the titanic struggle you're going to experinece as you progress through this program.

It's the Battle of The Boss vs. The Bitch

CHAPTER 11

THE BOSS VS. THE BITCH: THE EPIC BATTLE OF 75HARD

The subtitle of this book is "A Tactical Guide to Winning the War With Yourself."

The reason that's the subtitle is that there is definitely a war going on in life.

It's a war with yourself.

Every day...there is an epic battle going on inside you.

It's the battle between two voices in your head.

I call them The Boss Voice and The Bitch Voice.

The Boss Voice is the one that speaks to us of our potential for greatness.

It's the voice that drives us to better ourselves, to become the best we can possibly be.

It's the voice that we hear (and obey) whenever we choose to take an action that sharpens our discipline, increases our confidence, or broadens our vision for what is possible.

The Boss Voice will sound like a drill sergeant sometimes. It will speak to you clearly and powerfully, won't mince words, and will tell you what's up!

It will bark at you to stop whining, stop making excuses, get off your ass, and get to work!

But the Boss Voice can also sound like your best friend and biggest ally, who believes you're The Shit and doesn't hesitate to tell you that!

You probably know the scenario where you've had a couple of beers, you walk into a restroom, look at yourself in the mirror, and think, "Damn! I look good! Why wouldn't anyone want to get with me?"

Yes! That's the Boss Voice cutting loose and having a little fun. That's the Boss Voice slapping you on the back and saying, "Celebrate! You earned the right to feel good about yourself!"

The Boss Voice is always positive, always pushing you forward, always challenging you go hard after who you want to be and what you want to do.

If everyone listened to their Boss Voice, the human race would be filled with far more exceptional men and women than it is right now. Each of us would accomplish amazing things. We'd discover cures for fatal diseases. We'd invent ways to travel around the world in less than an hour.

We'd perform physical and mental feats like nothing anybody has ever seen before. To borrow a phrase from my friend Dr. Joe Dispenza, we'd "become supernatural."

The problem is, most people don't listen to their Boss Voice.

They listen to the other voice.

The Bitch Voice.

The Bitch Voice is the voice that speaks fear and doubt and discontent and rationalization and laziness into our minds and hearts. The Bitch Voice is a forked tongue demonic master sorcerer who knows exactly what lies we will believe and exactly how to talk us out of anything that would lead to us become truly great or to accomplish anything truly great. The Bitch Voice is cunning and knows exactly when to be direct with us and when to be subtle and sneaky, to distract us instead of discourage us.

When you say to yourself, "I want to lose 100 pounds," who do you think responds, "that's going to take forever"?

The Bitch Voice.

When you wake up to work out, who do you think immediately says, "It's so cold out this morning. Wait until later in the day when it's warmer"?

The Bitch Voice.

The Bitch Voice is the one who originates every fucking negative word that enters the human mind and goes out into human society.

It is the voice that practically trademarked phrases like:

"Not now."

"Maybe tomorrow."

"You can't."

"You shouldn't."

"Who do you think you are?"

"How dare you?"

The Bitch Voice is the mastermind behind every mindset or movement that makes every possible excuse for why a person can't become what they really want to become and do anything that they fucking want to do.

"You come from a shitty family."

"You were born into a lower economic class."

"You're a woman in a man's world."

"You're a minority in a white culture."

"You weren't born with the right genetics."

"You aren't educated enough."

Those are fucking terrible words and phrases, aren't they?

But let's be honest...you've heard those exact phrases in your head and, if you're like most people, you've not only heard them...

...you've obeyed them!

You've let them dictate your actions.

You've let them **CONTROL** you.

The really critical thing you have to understand is that the more you listen to one of the two voices, the stronger that voice will become in your head.

That's good news if you consistently listen to and obey the Boss Voice. That means the Boss Voice will get more and more and more powerful and **YOU** will get better and better.

But the bad news is that the vast majority of people don't listen to and obey the Boss Voice.

They listen to and obey The Bitch Voice.

And that's sad.

Really, it's more than sad...it's tragic.

There are tens of millions of human beings that could be living lives of confidence and freedom and happiness and success...and along the way contributing to their families, their communities and the world...even if "by only" setting a quiet example of what to follow for their kids...

...and they aren't.

There are so many amazing things that could be accomplished...

...and they won't be.

Because people are enslaved to their Bitch Voice.

And they don't know how to power up their Boss Voice.

Well...buck up, motherfucker!

Because the fact that you are reading this right now and have committed to 75Hard means that you are different.

You are about to learn how to silence the Bitch Voice and how to empower the Boss Voice.

In a way...if I had to simplify everything down to one basic principle, it's this:

You will create mental toughness when you learn to listen to and obey the correct voice.

That's exactly what 75Hard will teach you to do.

Every aspect of the program is designed for that purpose. And if you follow through with the requirements of this program—again, without compromise and without deviation **EXACTLY** as its prescribed in this book—you will achieve that purpose.

So now let's look in depth at the requirements of the program...

CHAPTER 12

THE HARD CORE: THE FIVE CRITICAL TASKS OF 75HARD

Every valuable program in the history of Earth that ever powerfully transformed people's lives had a core foundation that was well-thought out and carefully presented.

75Hard is no different.

What you're about to read is the foundation of the program that is going to help you cultivate mental toughness, so that you can become the person you want to be and do everything want to do.

Introducing...The Hard Core.

These are the 5 Critical Tasks that are at the heart of 75Hard.

Over & over again, on my podcast & at conferences & in personal conversations, I've told millions of people that success is pursuing your own full potential and that the key to that pursuit is (1) identifying the critical tasks that need to be done every day and (2) completing those critical tasks.

At the center of the 75hard program are Five Critical Tasks that need to be completed every day.

Before I tell you *what* the 5 tasks are, I need to tell you *how* they need to be completed.

1. The five critical tasks need to be completed every day for 75 days straight. Am I repeating myself? Yes. Will I continue to repeat myself throughout this book? Absolutely. Why? Because I have learned that people need the truth drilled into their heads again and again and again until they understand it and commit to it. So let me be very clear and let me repeat myself:

These five tasks need to be completed every day before you go to sleep. I don't care if you go to sleep at 8:00 p.m. or 1:07 a.m. All five critical tasks need to be completed every day. Before you go to sleep. For 75 Days straight.

If you miss even one day, you have to start over at Day 1.

Did you catch that?

If you miss even one single Hard Core Critical Task, you have to start over.

If you miss even one task on day 74, you have start over on Day 1...which lots of people have done by the way.

2. The Five Critical Tasks need to be completed exactly how I tell you to complete them.

In other words, you cannot tweak or adjust the requirements of any of the tasks for any reason.

You cannot say, for instance, "well, I'm married and have three kids. I have less time available than a single person. So I'll just workout each day for 30 minutes instead of 45 minutes." No. Not allowed. You can't say "I'll commit to five critical tasks every day for 75 days, but I'm going to personalize it to my goals. It'll be "My 75 Hard." No. There is no such thing as "My 75Hard" or "Your 75Hard." There is only 75Hard. You complete the five tasks set forth exactly as the program prescribes, or you aren't doing 75Hard.

You are in fact doing #75IBitchedOut.

The fact that you even think about changing it is exactly the sort of problem 75 Hard will cure you of: Adjusting situations in life to make them more convenient for you and justifying it as better for "your situation" ...instead of admitting the truth...you're being a lazy fuck.

In just a moment, you'll find out what the five critical tasks of 75Hard are. You'll also learn my rationale for choosing each task. But here's what you need to understand before that:

First, if you are going to cultivate mental toughness, you need to know how to follow through with a plan *to the letter*. You have to know how to follow directions *to the letter*. You have to learn how to execute on what you intend to do, with no wavering. No deviation. No substituting. No justifying. No tweaking. **NO MATTER WHAT.**

ZERO FUCKING COMPROMISE.

The reason I am 1000 percent inflexible on this is that adaptations and deviations and "little tweaks" are always a response to someone thinking that the situation isn't ideal and conditions aren't perfect. So they feel like they have to adjust to the situation, to compensate for imperfect conditions.

If you have that attitude, and most people do, guess what happens?

That adjustment, that deviation, that substitution opens the door wide open for justifying why you "just can't do" [fill in the blank].

And that justification leads to *compromise*.

And I guarantee you, if you *compromise* your intention and commitment, it won't be long before you *quit...anything.*

I guarantee it!

I've seen it in my own life.

I've seen it in the lives of thousands and thousands of other men and women.

It is a fact, and here's what you need to understand: The situation will never be perfect. Conditions will never be ideal. You need to be able to effectively operate **ESPECIALLY** when conditions aren't ideal... because that's most of the time.

If you allow yourself to respond differently to various conditions, you'll be the guy who sets out to do X, runs into obstacles and annoyances he didn't expect, and ends up quitting after three weeks...or three days.

Sound familiar?

Then what happens?

You crawl up on your couch, pop in Pacific Rim 3, and do nothing but stuff your fat face with Doritos and hate yourself for the rest of the year.

So there are no compromises allowed in this program.

Zero.

Not even a .00001 percent adjustment of the requirements.

The second you compromise the exact requirements of 75Hard is the second you are no longer doing the program. You have disqualified yourself and, if you want to keep going, you need to start over from Day 1.

Second, if you are going to cultivate mental toughness, you need to know how to master the monotonous.

You know what monotony is, right? One definition is "wearisome uniformity or lack of variety."

My definition is: "the boring shit you ruin your whole life (unsuccessfully) attempting to avoid."

I guarantee you, that as valuable as the 5 Critical Tasks of 75Hard are, at some point in the 75 days, after you've done the same 5 things day after day, you're going to say, "man, this is monotonous. This shit is boring me."

Too bad.

In life, it's the boring shit you have to do to get where you want to be.

I'm talking about the not even remotely glamorous or exciting regular tasks you have to perform every day to move one step closer to personal and professional success, closer to achieving all your goals and dreams.

You have to master the monotonous in order to become the ruler of your daily routine, which in turn leads to you literally being able to accomplish anything you set your mind to.

It's hard. It's rarely fun. But there is no other proven process for producing exceptional success.

I use the word "exceptional" because that's what you'll be if you master the monotonous.

You will become an "exception" to the rule.

You'll be an outlier. An overachiever. A god among mortals.

You know why?

The rest of the crowd is addicted to ease and excitement.

They don't want to accept the fact that the road to achievement and success is often monotonous. They want to think that the experience of pursuing success is like a montage from a movie.

You know what a montage is, right?

It's a series of short scenes that all have a common theme and basically summarize part of a movie plot.

Most of the time, when you watch a montage in a movie, there's some badass motivational song playing in the background.

Here's an example from an old school movie, Rocky IV. The montage is supposed to show us how Rocky trained to fight the bad Russian dude and it goes like this:

- Rocky arrives in the cold Russian countryside
- Rocky trains in an old farmhouse
- Rock jumps rope faster than anyone alive
- Rock performs amazing feats of strength
- Rocky runs up the side of a fucking mountain
- Rocky lifts his fists toward the sky and lets out this primal yell

The whole time the scenes are playing, there's hard, motivational music playing. The whole montage takes about 2 minutes. It's pretty neato.

But it's not reality!

Real life isn't a montage.

There aren't quick scenes that shift from one moment to the next. There's no motivational music playing in the background.

Real progress in real life takes a whole lot longer to develop. Real life doesn't zip by in rapid succession; it unfolds in slow, steady progression that is often painstaking and painfully dull.

I know...that kinda sucks...but the minute you realize and accept it as truth your life will change dramatically.

You don't learn to compete or achieve success through a movie montage.

You compete and you achieve by mastering the monotonous. It takes ongoing commitment, relentless focus, and time. If you try to tackle it all at once you are going to fail.

That's why 75Hard requires you to do the same five critical tasks.

And why you have to do the same five critical tasks exactly the same way.

Every day.

Day after day.

For 75 Days.

Yes, that's hard.

Really fucking hard.

But do you want to be happy or not?

Do you want to be successful or not?

Do you want to take quantum leaps forward in the pursuit of your own full potential or not?

Do you want to accomplish things you never thought possible or not?

Do you want to become the type of person that other people literally dream about or not?

I don't know about you, but I do.

I want to leave a legacy behind me.

I want to be a fucking Legend.

You know who was a legend and understood that, in order to become that, you had to master the monotonous?

Bruce Lee.

Remember Bruce Lee? He was the most badass martial arts master of all time.

He said, "I don't fear the man who has performed 1000 kicks 1 time, but the man who has performed 1 kick 1000 times!"

That's it.

Mental toughness is the result of the constant, unflinching completion of monotonous critical tasks.

Happiness is built on the relentless repetition of character-building habits.

Success comes from doing the boring, but essential shit every day.

EVERY. FUCKING. DAY.

75Hard is going to require that you build the skill of mastering the monotonous.

So tattoo that principle on your mind and heart and **WILL.**

Third and finally, you have to know your purpose for pursuing mental toughness

A lot of people talk about mental toughness and they say, "I'd like to be mentally tough," but they never ask themselves the question, "why?"

Why do you want to be mentally tough? Now, above all, I think the ultimate purposes can be "I want to be successful and happy." But in your own life, you have to be more specific than that. You have to have a specific purpose and constantly remind yourself of that purpose.

Why? Because it takes a lot of work to become mentally tough.

It takes a lot of time and a lot of energy. And if you don't really know why you are doing it...

...you won't follow through...just like all the other times.

So figure out what your purpose is. You don't have to overthink it, either.

Your purpose might be "I want to be rich as fuck."

Your purpose might be "I want to look like The Rock."

Your purpose might be "I want to have more confidence with women (or men)."

Your purpose might be "I have a high stress life and I want to handle it in the best way possible."

Your purpose might be "I want to set a better example for my kids and give them the best possible roadmap to follow in life so they don't end up being hunks of shit"

To help you come up with your specific purpose, think about your personal vision for your life.

Who do you want to become?

What do you want to accomplish?

You can become even more specific and breakdown your life into three categories: personal, professional, and physical. What's your vision for your life in each of these three area?

Do you want to make 6,7 or 8 figures year?

Do you want to have confidence to meet and marry the person of your dreams?

Do you want six pack abs?

Whatever your purpose is, take time to actively visualize that purpose.

Vividly picture in your mind what you are trying to achieve.
The practice of visualization isn't just for realizing your dreams.
It is a key to becoming mentally tough.

How so?

Because vision drives discipline.

Ask yourself this: why would you want to do something hard,
unless it resulted in something you really, really wanted?

Nobody with a brain in their head is out there just punishing themselves
for the sake of punishing themselves...except the few that "get it" (...and
after 75 days I promise you'll be among that few...no matter how far away
from the "current you" that sounds).

So what's your purpose?

What is it that drives you?

Why do you really want?

What is it you really need?

You need to constantly identify that purpose because, like I said, vision
drives discipline. You won't put in the work to create mental toughness
unless you are clear on why you're working so hard.

Okay...so with all that being said...let's talk specifically about each of the
Five Critical Tasks.

CHAPTER 13

CRITICAL TASK #1
CHOOSE A DIET AND COMMIT TO IT
(WITH THE GOAL IN MIND TO IMPROVE YOUR HEALTH AND PHYSIQUE)

If you asked the average person to identify one area of their life where they lacked discipline, a good number would answer "food."

We all know the statistics. About forty-percent of Americans are obese. Even though that's not a majority, that's still a huge number. But in my opinion and experience, that fact doesn't come close to representing how bad the situation is when it comes to most people's relationship to what they eat.

As a guy who has struggled with my weight my whole life, I know how it feels when a person who is born with a fast, efficient metabolism looks at you, points a finger, and says, "what's wrong with you? How hard is it to just not overeat and not be fat? Have some self-respect!"

My first response is: "*fuck you*. You have no idea how difficult it is for people like me, who could literally do nothing more than *smell* a deep dish, Meat Lovers Pizza—and gain ten pounds."

Is that you? I get it. Trust me.

But my second response is, over-eating is just *one way* that people fail to exercise discipline in their relationship with food.

As a guy who runs a nutritional supplement empire and works at the heart of the fitness industry, I can tell you this:

A ton of people under-eat...and that's why they lack energy and stamina.

A ton of people eat the right volume of food, but not the right combination....and that's why they aren't operating at peak performance.

A ton of people have never actually taken the time to determine whether or not they have dietary allergies...so they don't realize that there's something they are eating that is specifically causing inflammation...

...and causing fatigue, brain fog, ...

...or just plain causing them to feel like shit.

And since that old saying is a scientific fact— *"you are what you eat"*— dysfunction and deficiencies in your diet means dysfunction and deficiencies in you.

You will never get what you want out of yourself until you get control of what you put into yourself. Period.

That's why the first critical task of the 75Hard program is focused on you and your relationship with food. I wanted to zero in on something that is not only fundamental to your actual existence, but something that you have to face every single day of your life.

Every single day you feel the need for food.

Every single day you feel a desire for certain kinds of food—some of which are good for you, some of which aren't.

Every single day, you face choices—decisions—related to food.

Every single day, at the end of every day, you can look back and ask yourself, "Were those choices good choices? Or did they suck? Did they help move me toward who I want to be and the life I want to live? Or did my choices move me away from my ideal self and life?"

There is literally no other area of life where you are daily...hourly... constantly being faced with decisions and choices that have such a profound effect on your experience of life. For this reason, when it comes to your existence at its most basic level, there's no area of life that is most critical for you to exercise discipline and mental toughness.

So that's why the first critical task focuses on your diet. You need to exercise mental toughness when it comes to what you eat.

But before you misunderstand, let me clear about something:

In this program, I'm not going to tell you what you should eat. I'm not giving diet recommendations.

The reality is, every human being is different. We have different genetics, family dynamics, work environments, lifestyle features, time schedules, you name it. So I'm real skeptical about any diet book that claims to be a one-size-fits-all.

The truth is, if you really care about your health, and if you want to live life at peak performance, you need to take the responsibility yourself to figure out what your diet should be.

That's right. *You* have to do it.

How do you that?

It's real simple.

1. Get your goals set. Where do you want to be physically? Are you overweight and need to lose pounds? Do you feel like you're too skinny and need to add muscle? Do you need to build strength to deal with the physical requirements of your work or life? Those are critical questions. What are your goals?

2. Get some help. I believe 100 percent in taking personal responsibility and ownership of your life. But that doesn't mean I think people should go it alone. Especially when it comes to our health, most of us need help. Find a personal trainer or fitness professional who will consider your goals and help you determine what your diet should be. (My own company offers this for free, if you'd like to check it out: mytransphormationstartstoday.com.)

Like I said...that's up to you! And you need to get that all figured out *before* you start 75Hard.

But once you do...

Once you have determined what your goals are...

...and once you've determine what your diet should be...

...that's when you're ready to start 75Hard.

...and the very first task is to commit to that diet.

People have a hard time understanding what commitment really means, so let me spell it out for you.

Commitment means unwavering consistent execution. That means you have to commit and keep to this diet, every single day, for 75 days. No days off. No mornings off. No afternoons off. No evenings off. No hours off. No minutes off. 75. Days. Straight.

Commitment means no switching up the diet for a break or a change of pace or any other reason. That means no cheat meals. It means no "re-feed" meals. It means not even one unauthorized *M&M* or *Gummi Bear* or strawberry milk shake.

It also means that if you're supposed to get **IN** a certain number of calories or protein, and you think...*I'm just sick of eating so much chicken...* too bad. You can't decide to skip that meal.

Commitment means that you are holding yourself to this diet to the letter, not giving yourself flexible categories that you can manipulate when you feel like it. If you are on a "macro based diet" (which is a ridiculous term because literally every diet is Macro based)... you are not allowed to justify shitty food because it fits your macros. It's not allowed for 75Hard. (If you aren't familiar with the counting macros approach, it basically means someone can say, "Well, I've got a daily budget of x grams of carbs and I haven't used them, so I can justify eating this piece of pizza because I'll still stay within my daily allowance!"... if you are following a "macro" program the food must be clean...no junk.

You need to determine ahead of time specifically what your diet is going to look like and follow it exactly. So, for instance, you might have a daily diet that looks like this:

Meal 1

1 cup of egg whites
½ cup of gluten free quick oats

Meal 2

6 oz. ground turkey (93 percent lean)
3 oz. sweet potato
100 grams of vegetables (green beans)

And so on...

Get it?

Look, I'm not saying there can't be some variety, for instance, in your protein source. It's okay to sometimes eat lean turkey, sometimes eat fish, sometimes ground beef. But it's imperative that you set those parameters ahead of time. You just can't take the fluid, arbitrary, "counting macros" approach. That won't work for 75Hard because it allows for too much deviation, which as I explained earlier, is what leads to compromise and quitting.

The other thing—and I wish I didn't have to say this, but some people don't have any common sense—is that I understand that there may be marginal, insignificant discrepancies in the amount of food you eat. For instance, one food scale might register a handful of green beans as 50 grams, while a different scale identifies it as 53 grams. So technically, depending on the scale, you might eat more or less food than you were "supposed" too. If that happens, don't make a big deal about it. There's no way to avoid these variances. Use your head.

The point is to be committed. To keep to the diet *you* determined ahead of time.

And on some level, you're just going to have to apply a little common sense. You know when you are doing something you aren't supposed to. **Don't do it. The program won't work if you do.**

So at this point, I hope you understand something critical, something I really want to drive home:

The 75Hard program doesn't dictate and demand a particular diet.

I'm not telling you what to eat.

What it does require is that you commit to a diet.

What I am telling you is that once you choose what you're going to eat, there can be zero compromise and zero deviation.

You have to commit to it 100 percent.

For 75 days straight.

75. Days.

Got it?

Good.

But there's one more thing that 75Hard requires, when it comes to your diet.

Commitment means *no alcohol.* Listen, I love a good beer as much as the next guy. I understand that wine in moderation has health benefits. But the reality is, for the average person, alcohol has zero health benefits and, in most (if not all) cases, works against their health. But that's not why this is a requirement of 75Hard. It's a requirement because (1) most people really enjoy drinking (2) drinking almost always goes hand-in-hand with over-eating and over-indulging ourselves and (3) giving up drinking is a lifestyle adjustment, is hard, and requires mental toughness. That's what we're working to cultivate, so that's why no alcohol is allowed!

So to wrap this up...

Choose a diet.

Commit to it.

When we first launched the 75Hard program, some participants protested that they were alcoholics & couldn't go 75 days without drinking. I cannot & will not provide professional advice to you. But I will say this: if you can't give up alcohol right now, this program isn't for you. This is for people who are serious about becoming the best version they can be. That said, *Alcoholics Anonymous* recommends that, when you start their program, you attend 90 straight daily meetings. Why not get serious about your recovery, start going to meetings, & work 75Hard into your program?

100 percent.

No compromise.

No deviation.

75 days straight.

That's task #1 of 75Hard.

Note: As crazy as it sounds, there are "experts" and "gurus" out there who have never actually participated in or completed their own programs. I would never ask you to do something I had not done myself. Not only because that's unethical, but because I wanted to (1) make sure this program actually worked and (2) experience its power in my own life.

So with that being said...

In this "What I Did" part of the discussion of a critical task, I just share informally what I did personally as I was working through the 75Hard program.

As I progressed through 75Hard, I kept a journal, and even had my team record interviews with me, where I talked about how I handled different issues that came up as I worked to complete the daily requirements.

This is me getting real & practical & tactical about my experience, & I know it's going to help you!

WHAT I DID FOR CRITICAL TASK #1

So this is what I did when it came to choosing a diet and sticking to it:

I went the first 10 days on a Ketogenic diet. That means a diet with no carbs. The reason that I chose a Ketogenic diet is because in a Ketogenic diet, you cannot cheat on it or else you have to start all over again. Once you eat a reasonable amount of carbohydrates on a Keto diet, you get bumped out of ketosis. So there's a period of time where you have to adhere to the diet 100% or it won't work at all. In fact, not only will it not work,...it'll actually be counterproductive.

So, what I did was I made the first 10 days completely Ketogenic.
I modified a traditional ketogenic program and I ate high protein, moderate fat, and zero carbs. (Traditional ketogenic programs are high fat, lower protein and zero/very low carbohydrate)

The reason I did that in the first 10 days was because I wanted to hone in on my momentum and discipline and I wanted to lock that in upfront before I introduced any kind of carbohydrates, or a different kind of diet because that requires a lot of discipline for me because, the reality is... I love carbohydrates. A lot.

I knew that I had to get my discipline locked in the first 10 days.
So I purposely made the first 10 days more difficult.

I knew I had to get myself used to not having carbs, so that, once I reintroduced them, it would almost feel as if I was cheating on my diet. (And that's actually what happened: the first 10 days were so tough that the last 65 days felt like a piece of cake!)

So after the first 10 days what I did is I went into a carbohydrate rotation diet, where I did one high carbohydrate day, one moderate carbohydrate day, one low carbohydrate day, and then one zero carbohydrate day.

For all of you who are interested in these kind of details: my macro counts were steadily 280 grams of protein, 80 to 100 grams of fat throughout the program with the carbohydrate amounts rotating **HIGH/MODERATE/LOW/ZERO** then repeat.

So on my high carb day, it was 150 grams of carbs.

On my moderate carb day, it was 100 grams of carbs.

 On my low carb day, it was 50 grams of carbs.

And then on my zero carb day, it was a zero carbs, just whatever trace amounts happened to be in green vegetables and foods like that.

So then, I maintained that diet plan the rest of the program.

Again, it's a four-day carbohydrate rotation
The reason I liked that diet is because, first of all, it works.

It keeps your body guessing, it keeps your body burning fat. And it gives your body enough fuel to perform

To some extent, I can't talk about Task #1 without referencing Task #3, because there's such a connection between diet and working out.

So that's what I'm going to do right now. I'm also going to quickly refer to some specific supplements I used that while not required are helpful.

*FULL DISCLOSURE:** Obviously I own a supplement company and yes I believe we make the very best products so that's what I used. This is not a pitch to become a customer of 1st Phorm, that would be amazing and we'd love to have you as part of the family, however if you have another favorite company you like...by all means use those products. There are a lot of quality companies out there to choose from.

However, if you are new to supplementation there are a lot of unscrupulous (to put it mildly) companies out there too.

Do your homework. Be an educated consumer.

Don't worry: at the end, I'll summarize the supplements, with some information about where to find them.

So, what I did was train in the morning with weights; and then I took my post-workout shake around 1:00 p.m... That shake was always a combination of 1st Phorm Phormula-1 protein with 1st Phorm Ignition.

Then I started my meals throughout the day, and I evenly spaced them out about every three hours until I went to bed.

So, basically I added an intermittent fasting component to my carbohydrate rotation program, because after I ate my last meal, which was around 11:00 p.m. to midnight, then I didn't eat again until 1:00 p.m. the next day.

So there was a 13-hour intermittent fasting window, which worked very well for my goals.

Now, obviously my goals were to burn fat and gain muscle and just improve my physique.

Some people are going to want to focus entirely on fat loss.

Some people are going to focus all on muscle gain. It just depends on the person.

The diet I committed to is probably not going to be the best diet for someone who's trying to only gain muscle as their main goal, but if you're trying to lose fat and get leaner, it's a fucking great program. It works.

So before I move on to other issues, let me give you a quick summary of my meals, as well as a rundown of the supplements I used:

TYPICAL MEALS:

Pre Lift: 1st Phorm MegaWatt and EvoGen Carnigen
(Evogen is a company owned by my great friend Hany Rambod whose products I also enjoy & trust)

LIFT 45 MIN-60MIN

MEAL 1:

Post-workout shake (calories)
- 1st Phorm Phormula-1
- 1st Phorm Ignition
- 1st Phorm Opti-Greens
- 1st Phorm Opti-Reds

All of the 1st Phorm supplements I personally used can be found at 1stphorm.com/75Hard

MEAL 2 (LUNCH)

Steak salad
- 6 oz steak, lettuce, salsa

MEAL 3-4

- Chicken breast/steak/fish – 6-8 oz
- Vegetables (on low carb day)
- Potato/rice (on a high carb day)

MEAL 5

Protein pudding

- 1st Phorm Level 1
- With water / Almond milk

Put it in the freezer for 10-15 minutes until it gets the consistency of pudding

Other daily supplements

- 1st Phorm GDA
- Micro Factor
- 1st Phorm 1-DB
- 1st Phrom Thyro-Drive
- 1st Phorm Full Mega

All of the 1st Phorm supplements I used can be found together at 1stPhorm.com/75Hard

So that's basically the nuts and bolts of my diet.

The important thing for people to understand is that, in 75Hard, once you have your first meal you want to eat every three to four hours, and make sure you have at least 20-30 grams of protein with each meal, because that's going to keep you in a muscle repairing state (muscle protein synthesis). That means that you'll be building and repairing muscle versus losing muscle. Your body can only be in what's called muscle protein synthesis or muscle protein breakdown. It's also called anabolic and catabolic.

From my experience, the goal of this program for most people is to burn as much fat, but also repair as much muscle as possible. Because if you burn fat and you're building muscle at the same time, you're going to get leaner & you're going to look & feel better.

A lot of people make the mistake of just trying to starve themselves to lose weight. I guarantee you that won't be able to do it on this program.

Not eating is not acceptable and will be extremely counterproductive for a lot of reasons in the long haul.

You have to eat regular food, and you have to stick with it and consume as many calories as you need to, because you will get so burnt out and so worn out as you progress through 75Hard that you won't be able to take it.

So it's very important that your diet, regardless of your goals, is balanced and smart; otherwise, like I said, the 75Hard program will just wear you out.

One of the best things about 75Hard forces you to come up with a truly smart, balanced, and sustainable diet.

You'll come to understand that all these trendy, flash-in-the-pan diets are total bullshit. If you haven't already done so, you'll create a new habit of eating in a certain way that's really healthy for you.

So...what about going out to eat? How did I keep to my diet when I did that? Here are a few helpful tips I discovered:

1. When I joined my friends at a bar, I ordered decaf coffee. I'm not a coffee drinker, but the reason I picked decaf coffee is that it would come out hot and take a while to cool, which meant it would take a while for me to drink it. I actually don't like the taste at all, but practically, it gave me a drink to hold, and psychologically kept my mind off of thinking I needed something else to drink—like beer.

2. Whenever I joined others at a restaurant, I always ordered a ketogenic, zero carb meal. I would do that even if I was technically on a high carb day. Because when you go out, most restaurants are not going to be super careful about keeping fat and oil out of their menu items. They put all kinds of extra seasonings and oils on their food to try to improve the taste. So I would always keep it simple and safe. I'd order a lean steak, fish, and green vegetables and salad.

So...did you notice something interesting about what I just shared with you? I told you that I went out to the bar & ate out at restaurants during 75Hard. In other words...I continued to be social.

This is a huge point I have to make: you **SHOULD NOT** cancel your social life during 75Hard.

In fact, avoiding these more challenging situations contradict the entire point of the program.

The point of the program is that you're supposed to develop the mental toughness...the discipline, the time management, etc....to progress through the program and continue to live your life as you would normally live it.

So you need to go to all the family events...you need to attend the important social events.

You need to celebrate Thanksgiving and Christmas and Easter... and **STILL** keep to the program.

You don't stop living in order to do 75Hard.

75Hard teaches you how to take your normal life to an exceptional, mentally tough level...but only if you welcome the challenges that you find along the way on this journey.

CHAPTER 14
CRITICAL TASK #2
DRINK A GALLON OF WATER PER DAY

A lot of your problems in life could be solved by drinking.

Not alcohol.

Water.

Listen...

My good buddy, Vaughn Kohler, is the co-host of my podcast, REAL AF. A lot of you guys know him as "The Pastor of Disaster" or a number of other amazing nick names we like to give him on the show.

For about a year, he complained to me that he was having problems concentrating, was short of breath, didn't sleep well, was tired all the time, and just didn't feel right.

"Drink more water," I told him.

He didn't do what I said.

Instead, he kept drinking coffee, diet coke, sweet tea, lemonade, and bizarre fermented energy drinks.

He also went to see a chiropractor, a pulmonologist, got a sleep study done, started wearing Breathe Rite strips, and got his testosterone checked.

Now, all of those are—to some extent—legitimate options when you want to feel better.

But none of them really helped him.

Then I noticed a change.

All of the sudden out of the blue Vaughn was different.

When he came into the office, he seemed more alert. Awake. Focused. He seemed to have more energy. He was in a better mood.

"Hey," he said to me, when I asked about it. "I spent all this money thinking the problem was complicated and it wasn't."

"I should have listened to you," he said. "I just needed to start drinking more water."

Yes. He should have listened.

But I'll give him some credit. It's a common mistake. He's not alone.

If the average person struggles with discipline when it comes to eating, it is equally true that people—across the board—don't drink enough water. The "experts" say that, at the very least, you need 8.5 cups of water for your body to function well. According to the studies, though, the average American consumes only 1.8 cups. That's barely 20 percent of the water a person is supposed to drink a day!

You can probably already wrap your head around why that is bad.

But here's what you need to understand: the facts are, even if you are **2 percent** short of the amount of water you're supposed to drink, you are technically dehydrated. And once you are in a state of dehydration, you are susceptible to the following:

- Fatigue
- Dizziness
- Difficulty concentrating
- Dry skin
- Muscle cramps
- Bad breath
- Mood swings
- Body aches
- Headaches

You think you're going to realize your own full potential and get the most out of your life when you are suffering from those symptoms?

On the flip side, though, water provides the power to be your best.

- It helps maximize your physical performance
- It helps increase your energy level
- It helps your brain perform better
- It protects you from physical and mental fatigue
- It keeps you from becoming constipating so you can quick get waste out of your system
- It helps you lose weight
- It helps regulate your mood

There's no question: water is absolutely essential to your health and performance. And let me be straight with you: you're going to need to do everything you can to maintain optimal physical energy and regulate your mood if you're going to cultivate mental toughness over the next 75 Days. That's why one of the tasks of 75Hard is focused on your water consumption.

But the reality is, my rational for including drinking water in the list of tasks isn't just for the sake of your health.

The truth is, water is central, not just to physical health, but to all of existence. Along with earth, wind, fire, and space, water is one of the main elements of the universe.

Throughout the history of humankind, water has been a powerful, meaningful symbol.

Pretty much every religion and philosophy in the history of Earth uses water to symbolize life itself.

The different religions and spiritual traditions – from Christianity to Buddhism – use water as a symbol for....

Purification.

Renewal.

Vitality.

Transformation.

In addition to this, water has two characteristics that are the reason why I wanted a water-focused task to be included in the 75Hard program:

First, it is used to clean things. You use water to wash messes off.

Second, it has the power to transition from liquid to a solid (ice) and even into a vapor.

So what does all this have to do with 75Hard?

You're about to undergo a purification.

You and your life are about to get the Ultimate Wash.

Undesirable traits like laziness, compromise, and passiveness are going to slowly, steadily drained away.

You're going to experience new things in yourself and it's going to open up a whole new way of living, thinking and being.

You're going to feel healthy and alive in a way you never have before.

There's going to be a change in you and your life that's as real and elemental and significant as water changing from a liquid to a solid to a vapor.

So...

Not just health benefits.

But a symbol of a major transformation.

That's why drinking water is one the five tasks of 75Hard.

And not just drinking the recommended 8.5 cups a day.

In the 75Hard program, you are required to drink one gallon of water a day.

That's 16 cups. *Double what you need.*

Here's why:

• You'll be working out every day. Athletes need more water than average people because athletes perform at higher physical levels than most people. In the next 75 days, so will you.

• It requires planning and work. A gallon of water a day is way more than the average person drinks. So for the average person to fulfill this task, it's going to demand they put some thought and effort into it. Most people let the day slip by without doing what they need to do to stay hydrated. That can't happen in 75Hard. You have to stay on top of it.

So to bring this all together, I chose drinking 1 gallon of water a day as the critical task #2, not just because of the health benefits (this isn't primarily a fitness challenge, remember?) but because:

1. It will be a constant, symbolic reminder that you are undergoing a purification and transformation. As you push through the 75 days, this task is going to be a daily reminder of why you are doing this! And trust me, you're going to need that. In the midst of the grind, as your body aches and your mind fights the Bitch Voice, you're going to need to tap into the power of symbolism and the deeper, higher reason you are putting yourself through so much hard work. (Hell, you might even consider saying the words "I'm being purified" and "I'm being transformed" every time you take a drink...or at least think it to yourself so you don't get thrown in the looney bin).

2. It's going to take some real intention and effort on your part. It's going to keep you from getting complacent about your water intake and, by definition, keep you out of your comfort zone. And that's the key to cultivating mental toughness.

One gallon of water. Per day. That's the task. That's the requirement.

I don't care how you do it.

I don't care if you carry around a 1 gallon jug and sip from it throughout the day.

I don't care if you carry around eight 17-oz bottles of water.

I don't care if the water is lukewarm.

I don't care if it's ice cold.

But whatever happens, you must drink at least a gallon of water every day. Before you go to sleep for the night.

Oh...What's that? You got 7/8ths of a gallon in? Start over at Day 1: Zero Compromise.

WHAT I DID:

Before I talk about what I did when it came to making sure I got in the required gallon of water, I want you to go back and re-read the health benefits of being fully hydrated. I can't stress this enough: water intake is hugely important.

So different people have different ways they drink the water throughout the day, but for me, I started off drinking just regular bottled water which was fine.

It comes in 16.9 ounce bottles. So I always knew how many I needed to drink a day to hit one gallon.

About day 40 I switched to using a half gallon jug. I drank a minimum of two of these a day. I didn't get fancy, I just filled it up off a tap twice a day and drank it.

Out of the two methods I definitely found the ½ gallon jug the easiest, most convenient way to get in my water.

Other people might do it differently.

Some people might carry around a gallon milk jug that they filled with water. Others might carry around a half gallon or quarter gallon plastic drinking bottles. A lot of the customers who patronize my company use their 1st Phorm Grab n' Go Shaker as their water bottle, because it's sturdy, has a tight cap on it, and you can fill it up to 28 ounces of water. For those interested in doing the same, I'll put the information below. But really, it's whatever works for you!

As far as timing, I always drink 32 oz before I go to the gym in the morning, and I try to get all of my water in before 6:00 or 7:00 p.m.

The quicker you get the water in you, the quicker you get your metabolism going, and the more energy and focus you'll have for the day. Plus, who wants to be trying to drink a whole gallon of water in the evening, and then have to get out of bed multiple times because you're pissing all night?

• 1st Phorm Grab N Go Shaker

https://1stphorm.com/gear/accessories/water-bottles/1st-phorm-grab-n-go-shaker-black

CHAPTER 15
CRITICAL TASK #3
WORKOUT TWICE A DAY FOR
45 MINUTES EACH

Everybody who has devoted a significant amount of their lives exercising knows that what happens in the gym parallels what happens in the world outside of it.

If you go into it with good intentions and a good plan and execute that plan daily, good things happen.

If you work hard, you get results.

If you don't, you don't.

If you're careful and pay attention to the details, the gains will be significant and come quicker.

If you're sloppy and careless, you're going to end up like 99% of people who go to the gym and never look any different.

If you concentrate and focus on yourself, you get so much more out of yourself.

If you spend time distracted and comparing yourself to others, you're going to waste your time.

If you hit it hard every once in a while, you get nothing.

If you hit it on a regular basis, consistently, you'll gain everything you want.

Bottom line: What happens in the gym is what happens in life. It's directly parallel.

In my own life, deciding to make exercise and working out a lifestyle had a transformative effect on me.

As you've already read in this book, growing up I was the fat kid who only wanted to gorge himself on hot pockets and Twizzlers and gulp down Dr. Pepper. I put garbage in my body, I felt like garbage, and people treated me like garbage.

But because I had parents who would never let me sit on my ass and do nothing, but made me do chores that were damn hard for a kid, I learned how to do physical labor early in my life. I learned how to sweat. And like I told you earlier, my dad pushed us, not just to work hard, but to compete hard.

So when high school finally came around, I was ready for the physical training required to succeed in sports. As I went from a freshman to a senior, I didn't just learn how to exercise right. I learned to love working out—well, at least to love the results of working out.

The change that someone goes through—not just physically, but mentally—when they really commit to the gym is pretty amazing.

Ultimately, that's why I went into the nutritional supplement business. I love witnessing the massive transformations.

What I always found to be the most amazing to me was that the changes in people's bodies was NEVER the most profound transformation that occurred….it was the transformation of their minds and subsequently their lives.

The improvements in their biceps, abs, or calves—these were just surface level evidence that a much deeper change had occurred.

Ultimately, they had better bodies because they had become better people.

That's the first reason I'm making working out one of 75Hard's required tasks.

Again, remember that 75Hard is not at its core a physical challenge program. With that being said, mental transformation and physical transformation go hand-in-hand. As your body starts looking better and better, it will be a sign that there are real changes going on in your mind, too.

I want you to be able to look at yourself in the mirror and "see" the changes taking place in your mindset.

Bottom line: when your shape changes, it means your mind's getting into shape.

You're definitely going to get in way better shape in the next 75 days.

Because this is specifically what you are required to do.

1. Workout twice a day for 75 days straight. As with the other tasks, I'm not going to micromanage exactly what you need to do in your workout. Meaning, I'm not going to tell you that you have to do a specific set of exercises, or that you have to do five sets of x type of weight exercises, or that have to do a certain number of HIIT sessions a week.

But what I am going to insist on is that you work out twice a day, and that you don't do your workout back-to-back.

As you will discover, 75Hard is going to help you with discipline and organization and time management. It is actually designed so that you can't do a weight workout at 8:00 a.m. and then immediately follow it up with a cardio workout, just for the sake of convenience.

That's too easy...it's not #75CUPCAKE...its #75HARD. If you lift weights in the morning, you have to do cardio in the afternoon or the evening. If you lift weights at noon, you should do cardio no earlier than late afternoon. A good rule of them is to separate the workouts by at least 3-4 hours.

And remember: you need to do this every day for 75 days straight.

Every. Day. (No, you do not have to lift weights...that's what I did and **I HIGHLY RECOMMEND** some sort of resistance training as one of your workouts...but it's not required)

1. Each workout must be a minimum of 45 minutes. Repeat: each workout must be a minimum of 45 minutes. Not 43. Not 44. 45! And it has to be 45 minutes all at once. For instance, no spreading out 10-15 minute cardio workouts throughout the day.

That's two separate workouts. 45 minutes each. Got it?
ZERO COMPROMISE.

2. One of the workouts must be outdoors. You know the problem with indoor workouts? The conditions are controlled. 75Hard requires that you workout outside once a day, because you can't control the conditions.

The weather could be good. The weather could be bad. It could be mild & pleasant, or hot as hell. It could be cool & crisp or it could be frigid as Antarctica.

There might not be a cloud in the sky, or it could be a downpour. Doesn't matter. In life, conditions are never going to be perfect, and the mentally tough understand this. You still have to get your workout in.

And that's my second reason for requiring two 45-minute workout a day (one outside). It's just so damn inconvenient. By having to complete this requirement every day, in exactly the way I've said to do it, you're going to have to get good with your time.

You're going to have to become far better at managing your day, and you're even going to have to learn how to adapt and figure out how to get these two workouts in, when your day doesn't go as planned.

This will require that you start developing skills of time management, prioritization, adaptability, discipline, and persistence.

It will require you to cultivate mental toughness!

Nothing forces you to be more mentally tough than when conditions are less than ideal at best and out of control at worst.
So prepare yourself to get the work done, rain, shine, snow, sleet, heat...

ZERO COMPROMISE.

(By the way, here's me telling you again to use common sense: if lightning is flashing dangerously close to you or there's a tornado ripping through your town, then no...you probably shouldn't workout outside or wait for it to pass. My lawyers are making me say this by the way...get your shit done.)

That said, I think it's safe to say that weather conditions will rarely be so bad that your personal safety is in question and you shouldn't workout. So no excuses! I honestly don't care what workout you do outside. You can lift weights outside. You can do cardio. You can do a CrossFit workout. *I do not care.* I don't even care if you want to drag your treadmill or elliptical machine outside. I've done that myself many times.

Just do it. And do it outside.

Want to develop some mental toughness...go do your shit when literally **NOBODY ELSE** would.

I'm sure you can connect the dots here...but in case you can't: How much different would your life be if when everyone else in the world quits...you press on. Think how valuable that is in all areas of your life.

WHAT I DID

When it came to working out, the two things I made it a point to do were:

1. I worked out first thing in the morning
2. I took pride in doing my outdoor workout in terrible conditions

When I say I worked out first thing in the morning, I mean that it was the very first thing I did when I left my house.

I run a bunch of companies and have a lot of important personal projects going on.

All of that takes a lot out of me. The last thing I want to do is to have to work all day and then hit the weights after I'm already wiped out. On top of that, when you exercise early in the day, there are all sorts of benefits: increased energy, better mental focus, and you're just in a better mood...as well as revving your metabolism up for the day which from my personal experience equals more fat loss.

So I hit the workout early. I train with weights and I train intensely. Not everybody is going to do weight training, but I highly recommend that whatever you do, you do it early.

I would also recommend that your workout involve some sort of resistance training, because you'll end up looking better at the end... and how we look and feel has a lot to do with how we perform so don't snooze on it...**IT MATTERS.**

In terms of how I train, I pretty much do a traditional six-day split.

I train shoulders first, then chest, then legs, then back, then arms, and then legs again. So I train legs twice and everything else once a week.

Sometimes during 75Hard I'd be really fucking sore. I was always sore... but some days I mean like can't get off the toilet sore.

So instead of doing weights, I would just do two cardio workouts.

That way, I could give my body an active rest day. You need to understand that this isn't cheating. People are confused about that. The requirement is two workouts---one indoor and one outdoor. But nowhere do I say you have to do weight training. And, the reality is, a lot of cardio involves some sort of resistance.

The bottom line is that this program is intense, but it doesn't promote stupidity: sometimes your body needs a break from the weights.

Another misconception is that doing cardio means you have to run for 45 minutes.

No. It doesn't mean that. You can walk. But it's always good to scale your cardio so that it challenges you. So for me, I put on a 35 lb. weight vest and walked in the area around my house—which is full of long steady steep hills. Trust me: it's a workout. Not just taxing on the heart, but on my whole body (**GOOD**).

So, like I said, in addition to working out earlier, I also took pride in having to do my outdoor workout in terrible conditions.

In terms of timing, there was a couple of times during my program where the day got away from me. I wasn't able to get my outdoor workout in until late, late into the night. I can tell you there was at least 10 times where I had to do my outdoor cardio, like literally in the middle of the night, between 12:00 AM and 2:00 AM.

I would be out on the driveway, on the bike, trying to keep myself from falling asleep. I'm not going to bullshit you. It sucked!

But the reality is, 45 minutes goes pretty quickly…& when you are done, you feel so fucking good about yourself. You have a sense of pride that, regardless of how much you didn't want to do it, you **DID IT!** That's what the program is about.

One day I had to get up 4am and workout with weights then spend the whole day at a speaking event, then host a VIP dinner after the speaking event. By the time I got done, it was almost midnight, and I was completely wiped out.

That's when my Bitch Voice (yes, I have one, too) spoke up and said, "Listen, you're exhausted. You've worked so hard today. Nobody would blame you if you punked out on your 75Hard requirement. And really, nobody even needs to know! Just say 'fuck it.'

Well, I didn't say 'fuck it.' Instead, I spoke back to my Bitch Voice and said, "**FUCK YOU.**" By that point, I had created the mental toughness strong enough to deal with that kind of temptation. That was the closest I came to failing. It was April 6th 2019. Yes I know the date because in hindsight that was the major turning point for me where I started to really believe in myself and where the "power came on" mentally as I like to say.

The other thing that happened for me is that, instead of trying to get out of doing the outdoor workout when conditions weren't right, I actually **WANTED** conditions to suck. I took pride in going outside and working out when the weather absolutely sucked.

My first 75Hard experienced stretched across the changing of the seasons.

So I had the privilege of doing outdoor workouts in the intense, oppressive heat and humidity of summer in the Midwest. However, I also had workouts in 9 degree freezing cold blizzard conditions, where I had to put on two pairs of sweatpants and two sweatshirts and put on a stocking cap and thermal gloves and even a fucking ski mask. But I did it.

And I felt like a badass for doing it.

Where I live in Missouri, during the summer, there are tornado warnings all the time and I still did my outdoor workout. I'm not telling you to do that. You probably shouldn't.

I'm telling you that to show you just how disciplined and determined you become on 75Hard. It will happen to you too. Even if you are thinking right now: "Man this dude is nuts". I promise after 20 days you don't even care what the conditions are like.
After 30 days you **WANT** them to be hard.

You'll see.

That attitude toward the outdoor workout is just one example of what happens to you mentally as you progress through 75Hard. What happens is that you start to crave those opportunities that separate the average from the exceptional. You look for those situations where everybody else is packing it in and going home, but you're getting out and doing the hard thing nobody else is willing to do.

You end up feeling like a god among mortals because you can see and recognize by the day in a very literal way the gap between you and everyone else widening.

That's something 99% of people on this earth will never experience.

CHAPTER 16

CRITICAL TASK #4
READ 10 PAGES OF A NONFICTION / ENTREPRENEURSHIP / PERSONAL DEVELOPMENT BOOK PER DAY

Have you ever read the short story, *The Bet?*

It's by a Russian guy named Anton Chekhov, and it's fucking amazing.

Here's a quick summary of the plot:

In 1870 a banker and lawyer are at party and the banker bets the lawyer two million rubles that the dude can't spend five years in solitary confinement. As in, completely isolated and alone for five years!

The lawyer accepts the bet, but raises the stakes. He says he'll stay in solitary for fifteen years.

The two men agree to the bet, and the lawyer moves into the banker's guesthouse. He can't have contact with any human beings at all, but what he can do...

...is read books.

Any books he wants.

Novels.

Philosophy.

Religion.

You name it.

Well, time passes and fifteen years are almost up, when the banker starts getting really worried. He realizes the lawyer is going to make it and that he'll have to pay him! And that is going to bankrupt him...ruin him!

He's gets so desperate thinking about it that he decides he is just going to murder the lawyer, to get out of paying him.

So he sneaks into the guesthouse while the lawyer is sleeping, and is ready to kill him, when he sees a note.

The lawyer had written the note, and in the note, he explains that he's going to leave the guesthouse five hours earlier than he was required to stay.

Five hours short of fifteen years!

I don't want to tell you everything about the story because I want you to read it for yourself.

But the bottom line is that the lawyer didn't feel like he needed— or wanted—the money anymore.

He had spent fifteen years reading every type of book on Earth.

He had spent fifteen years learning from some of the most amazing authors in the history of the planet.

And his life was completely changed.

He was completely transformed.

And he was so grateful for that fact, that he willingly lost the bet...

...and thanked the banker.

Listen...I love money as much as anybody.

I know the good you can do with money.

Pursuing wealth for the sake of impacting the world is absolutely something everyone should be proud to do. I am.

But this short story makes a really, really good point.

Books are extremely valuable.

Reading is an indispensable habit for people who want to be happy and successful.

The best reading engages the mind and the heart and makes you a better person. And the reality is, learning something—I mean, not just acquainting yourself with information, but mastering concepts and ideas—requires discipline and determination.

The brain is a muscle, just like any muscle. It gets tired when you work it. But when you work it, it grows!

So if you are truly committed to educating yourself more and more every day, that will—by necessity—demand that you become more focused, disciplined, and persistent.

If you're really committed to being a lifelong learner, it will be absolutely necessary to develop mental toughness!

So that's why I've made reading critical task #3 of 75Hard.

Every day, you are required to read 10 pages of a non-fiction / entrepreneurship / personal development book.

And let me unpack this for you so there's no misunderstanding:

1. "Nonfiction / entrepreneurship / personal development" means the following: first and foremost, you can't read a novel. You can't read a collection of poetry or short stories. Those types of books are valuable and have their place, but what we're zeroing in on with this task is literature that is literally, specifically designed to help you develop yourself—professionally or personally. Books that will make you a smarter, better person. Examples of great books on entrepreneurship would include titles like:

- Crush It by Gary Vaynerchuk
- The Purple Cow by Seth Godin
- Building a Story Brand by Donald Miller

Examples of great books on self-development would include titles like:

- The Lombardi Rules by Vince Lombardi
- The Magic of Thinking Big by David Schwartz
- Relentless by Tim Grover

(By the way, if you want a full list of my book recommendations, go to andyfrisella.com/badass books)

You also can't read articles from a magazine or hop onto the internet and read the daily post from your favorite blogger.

You **CAN** use a Kindle or Nook or some other eReader.

But you have to be reading a book.

10 pages a day.

Not 8. Not 9. 10 full pages.

(Common sense alert: I'm also assuming you understand that the book needs to be printed in a traditional format, with approximately 200-300 words a page, and that you're not reading ten pages of a book that has 5 words on each page, printed in 100-point font, coloring book or kids book.)

So to recap:

Read 10 pages of a non-fiction / entrepreneur / personal development book every day.

For 75 days straight.

2. Whatever book you begin to read; you need to finish. Then you can move on to another one. As a general rule of thumb, it's not bad to be reading several books at once. But for 75Hard, I want you to focus on one until you are finished. So it's important to do a little leg work and be fairly certain that

- You're going to get a lot out of it.
- You're actually going to enjoy reading it. But regardless...once you commit to starting the book, you have to finish it. When you do, you can move on to the next one!

3. You cannot fulfill the requirement by listening to audio books. The facts are, you will be more fully engaged when you have a book in front of you and you have to actually concentrate and read it. Listening to audio books is something that allows you to multi-task, and for the nature and purposes of 75Hard, it is considered cheating. Don't do it. "But Andy, I learn better through listening" ... that's you justifying an easier path...which we are going to put an end to forever over the next 75 days.

As you progress through 75Hard and experience so many changes and improvements, I guarantee you that adding to your knowledge through reading every day will end up being one of the most satisfying aspects of the program.

For those who aren't used to reading that much on a regular basis, it'll be a little bit of a chore at first.

But I promise you...on some level, you'll end up feeling like the lawyer in Chekhov's short story.

You'll feel transformed.

You'll feel grateful.

Bet on it!

WHAT I DID

I'll be straight with you: reading ten pages a day was easy for me because I'm a reader, anyway. I always read ten pages, so that was not something that was hard for me. The truth is, I'm a slow reader, but it's still easy for me to get 10 pages in. So this requirement was not a challenge for me. I'm not trying to brag about that, just being honest.

As I progressed through 75Hard, sometimes I knocked out the reading in my business partner Chris's office, sitting in my chair. Sometimes I did it at home, by the pool. Sometimes I started out my day by reading. There's really no best time to do it. It's whatever works for you. Just be sure to choose a time you're going to be awake and alert and can really process what you're reading.

Speaking of processing, one thing I want to point out is that reading well doesn't mean that you have to retain every bit of information you read. Hardly! Sometimes I will read a whole book and only remember one paragraph of information or insight...but that one paragraph can be **life-changing.** So I tell everyone to always be looking for that one paragraph, that one silver bullet of truth that you can take to improve your life
or business.

I will say that reading well does mean being an active reader.

Most people are passive readers. They just kick back, skim the page, look at their phone, turn the page, and eventually they "finish" the book. That's no good.

Instead, you want to be an active reader – which means you remove other distractions, to lock in on what you're reading, and you take notes.

If you're reading a traditional print book, you highlight key thoughts, write notes in the margin, and do anything else that helps you actively engage the material. If you're using a Kindle, that device has cool note-taking features—so use them!

I'm such an active reader that when I'm done culling the key points from a book, I'll actually create a Notepad file on my iPhone and input the information so that I can keep it permanently.

Then, from time to time, I can go back and review what I've read to bulk on my knowledge and understanding and a lot of times it sparks new ideas later that I end up finding useful in my life and business that I didn't pick up the first time through.

The bottom line is that you shouldn't be just reading for the sake of reading.

You shouldn't just be turning the page to punch the ticket and meet the daily requirement. You want your reading to actually help you become a better person, build a better business, and live a better life.

If you want a good list of badass books, you can find my book recommendation list online:

https://andyfrisella.com/pages/andy-frisellas-book-list-for-bad-asses

CHAPTER 17

CRITICAL TASK #5
TAKE A PROGRESS PICTURE EVERY DAY

When I was a little kid, I went to this carnival where there was this huge inflatable house with lots of rooms.

The guy running that attraction told us we had to walk through all the rooms of the house. He also told that, when we exited the house, he was going to ask us a question. If we got the answer right, we got a prize!

My buddies and I stepped into the house. The walls of the first room we entered were painted blue. The next room we entered the walls were painted blue. And the next room after that the walls were blue. Same for the next room. And same for every room after that!

There were dozens of rooms in the house and, in every room, the walls were painted blue—or so we thought.

When we got to the last room, the attendant was standing at the exit.

"So," he said, "here's the question! Answer it correctly and you'll win the prize"

"Okay," I said. "Go ahead."

He smiled. Actually, he smirked.

"What color were the walls in the last room?"

We looked at each other and laughed.

Was he serious?

We were guaranteed to get it right and win a prize!

"Blue," I said, speaking on behalf of my friends. "Now where's our prize?"

"Oh, I'm sorry," the man said. "wrong answer!"

Wrong? What the fuck!

Impossible!

We argued with this guy and accused him of being shady. But he pulled out a swatch of paint, pointed to it, and asked us, "what color is this?

"Green," I said.

"That's right," he replied. "Green."

Then he held the swatch up to the walls of the last room.

The color was identical.

It wasn't blue at all.

It was green.

We were dumb-founded.

We had no idea what happened.

We had no idea how we got the answer wrong.

We had no idea how we didn't notice the color change.

But I do now.

Here's what happened: as we walked from room to room, the color changed—but only by very small degrees. What is technically referred to as the hue, the saturation, the luminance...these components of color were adjusted in a very small, almost imperceptible way.

Actually, not "almost" imperceptible. Totally imperceptible!

In fact, the adjustments were so small that our minds didn't register a change at all!

We started off seeing blue and we never noticed any change.

The carnival dudes pulled a mind trick on us.

So we didn't win the prize!

Why do I tell you this story?

Because as you progress through 75Hard, there will be changes. There will be big changes. But from day to day, the changes will come in small, sometimes tiny adjustments.

Trust me, eventually you will notice them. But at first, you might not. At first, you might be so deep into the process that you can't, as they say, see "the forest from the trees." You'll be so deep into the details that you can't see The Big Picture.

Honestly, I wish there was some way to capture an image of your brain every day. An image that showed how your mindset, your attitude, your focus, your discipline, the resiliency of your thinking...how all that was transforming and improving. But unless you are a neuroscientist and have access to equipment that literally costs millions of dollars, there isn't.

So you have to do the next best thing: in 75Hard, you have to take a progress picture.

A picture that shows the physical results of your commitment to your diet, your 1 gallon of water, and that you are working out twice a day.

You need to take a picture like that. Every day.

By taking a progress picture every day, and having the opportunity to flip back and look at previous pictures, you will actually be able to see your progress. You'll be able to compare you on Day 25 to you on Day 1. You'll be able to see how much you've accomplished between Day 33 and Day 69.

That's the practical reason for taking a progress picture.

But like everything in 75Hard, my reasons go far, far deeper than practicality.

As much as everything I've just written is true and important, the ultimate reason that I require a daily progress pic is this: achieving progress and experiencing success can be so intoxicating that you forget that **what got you to that point in the first place was paying attention to the little details.**

See...when you get in the zone and start to improve all areas of your life & start to feel more powerful, you vision for your life gets bigger & you start looking for bigger & bigger tasks to accomplish.

And what happens is you forget that every single "big success" in your life is powered by a thousand "little" actions.

People totally forget this.

So they stop paying attention to the details. They let the little things slide. And because the little details are...well, *little*...they don't immediately notice the negative effect. It's barely perceptible. But before they know it, the effect of neglecting all those little details accumulates and—BAM—everything falls apart. A hairline crack in the dam, barely noticeable, leads to a flood of failure. So that's why I require something that seems so small and simple and insignificant as taking a daily progress pic.

People think it's the "easiest" task & not "as important" as the others. I've had people bitch at me, saying "Andy, I've absolutely crushed for 67 days, and you say I have to start over because I forgot to take the fucking progress pic? I can't see how it's that critical!"

My friend, that's why you are struggling in life. You aren't understanding the importance of small details.

So yes, you have to start over.

Because that's exactly the point: you can't "see" how critical the "small" tasks are. What you don't see...what you don't pay very close attention to...is exactly what will be your undoing.

So taking a progress pic is a daily, **ESSENTIAL** reminder of what it really takes to create mental toughness.

It's a daily lesson for what it takes to succeed at the highest levels. And the reason there is such a huge penalty for not completing that task in 75hard...the reason you have to start over from Day 1 no matter how much you crushed it up to that point...

...is that there is a huge penalty for not paying attention to the little details in ALL OF LIFE.

Think about it.

If you don't pay attention to the little details in your marriage—expressing gratitude for one another, doing kind things for each other on a daily basis, regularly communicating to make sure they are on the same page—you can find yourself divorced in no time.

If you don't get routine maintenance done on your car—little things that don't require a lot of work—it can lead to an expensive breakdown...& massive stress!

If you don't do little things to keep your house nice, the value of your home can plummet.

If you skip a workout here and there and add a couple "small snacks" thinking it's no big deal, the next thing you know...you'll be fat. Really fat!

If the coach of your favorite team doesn't take the time to break down the opponent's game film, your favorite team is going to get their ass kicked.

When NASA built the Challenger in 1986, they missed the "little detail" that an O-ring seal wouldn't function correctly in the kind of cold weather they had on the day of the launch. As a result, the shuttle exploded and seven crew members lost their lives.

I could on and on, but by now you've got the point.

The little details matter. Details are separators

Sometimes they aren't just the difference between success and failures.

Sometimes they are the difference between life and death!

Take a second to let that settle in.

I'm serious...before you keep reading, think about what I just wrote.

Got it?

Okay, so beyond the ultimate purpose of reminding you of the importance of paying attention to the little details, there are two other profoundly important reasons for requiring a daily progress pic:

The first reason I already touched on earlier, but I want to re-emphasize it because it's important: while you can't take a progress picture of your mind, taking a progress picture of your body will help to encourage you. You will know that you are developing mental toughness because you will see the physical results. You will be able to tell there is a transformation occurring in your mind because you will see the transformation happening in your body!

And trust me...you're going to need this. 75Hard is called 75Hard for a reason. It's fucking hard!

There will be multiple times that negative voice in your mind—the Bitch Voice—is going to say to you, "I can't do this.", "What's the point?", "This is unnecessary."

That's when you are going to look at your progress picture and say, "Shut up, Bitch. Of course I can do this. I see that I'm doing it!"

The Bitch Voice is going to want to lie to you. And every time it does, you're going to be able to point to the evidence—the progress pic—and say, "No. This is The Truth, The Whole Truth, and Nothing But The

Mother Fucking Truth."

At the same time, there's another reason for taking a progress pic that at first glance seems to be the exact opposite of what I literally just told you...about using the progress pic as proof against The Bitch Voice.

Here's what you'll discover: The more you progress, the more mentally tough you become, **you won't actually even need the progress pic to encourage and motivate you!**

You will come to the point where you look at the pic and acknowledge that there is progress being made, but you won't need it for validation.

I guarantee it will be a unique experience for you. It will be a highly rare combination of determination and detachment.

You'll care, but you won't care.

The reality is...it's the kind of phenomenon that only the truly elite experience!

Even people who are not basketball fans know that Michael Jordan is the greatest player of all time. Do you think he cared about his stat sheet? Yes. But just as one way of evaluating his performance. But do you think he needed to look at his stat sheet to validate himself? Hell no! When it came to one particular game or one individual stat column, he didn't give a fuck about "proving" anything. He knew the work he put in. He knew how driven he was. He knew that his will to win was a thousand times greater than any of his opponents. He had proved his commitment to himself again and again. He had perfect trust in himself. Supreme confidence.

Do you think The Rock cares about how many likes his posts get or how high his engagement on social media is? Again, yes. But only to evaluate, not to validate. Those are just clues to help guide him. They aren't even remotely critical to his confidence or his sense of who he is. He acknowledges the data. But he doesn't need it to know he's on the right path. Dwayne Johnson has proven over and over again that he can trust the promises he makes to himself & he will always follow through with his plans to excel at everything he does. He doesn't need my like or yours to convince him of that.

If you persevere through 75Hard and execute like you are supposed to, that's what will happen.

That's how you'll start to look at your progress pic.

You'll care, but you won't care.

It's a crazy feeling! It feels so good. You'll say "holy shit!" and "but I don't really give a fuck" at the same time. Trust me: it's unlike anything you'll experience in life.

But in order for that to happen, like I said...you have to take a progress pic. Every day. For 75 Days straight!

I feel like it should be pretty easy to understand how to do this, but let me walk you through it:

1. Just snap the photo using your cell phone. Who doesn't have a cell phone these days? Okay, if you don't, get a digital camera. Or use the Photo Booth on your Mac Laptop or whatever. Just find something that works to take the photo.

2. When you take the photo, make sure your body is visible enough people can see your progress. If you're a dude, take off your shirt and wear workout shorts. If you're a woman, you might consider wearing shorts or a swimsuit and a cutoff top or sports bra. Whether you're a man or woman, the point is to show skin so you can see how your body is changing and improving. And listen...there's no rule that says you have to post this progress pic on social media. You can if you want. But it's just for you. It's just so you can see your progress. So don't sweat it if you are shy or think you look bad.

(I will tell you this, though: I've learned that most people involved in fitness are actually good people who want to encourage others. There might be a hater or two. But most of the time, if you show the courage to post a progress pic publicly, people will be inspired by that and really provide positive feedback. Bottom line, though: it's up to you!)

3. Find a place to store all the photos so you can look back, compare the days, and see your progress. The easiest thing is to just create a 75Hard folder on your phone and store the photos there. But if you want to email them to yourself or upload them to iCloud or Google Photos, that will work too. Whatever works for you!

If you really commit to 75Hard, you're going to experience life-changing progress—mentally and physically. I guarantee it. But it's imperative to document that progress. And that's why it's required!

So take a progress pic.

Every day.

For 75 Days straight.

WHAT I DID

As far taking a progress pic, I did it at the end of the night. But I always set an alarm on my phone, and had my wife Emily set a reminder on her phone, too, because I didn't want to forget.

In spite of that, there were a couple times where I got into bed and suddenly realized, "oh shit! I didn't take my pic!" So I got up and did it. Because, like I said, taking the progress pic is important. Not doing it would send me—and you—back to Day 1.

As far as keeping track of my progress through the pics, I didn't really put any stock into that. I didn't really care how good I looked after 20 days or 40 days or whatever. I didn't really care. In fact, I didn't look at the pictures for almost the whole program. I had my wife Emily take the pictures and put them in her phone.

I did look at a few pics much later on in the program, compared them to earlier photos, and yeah—the results were ridiculously dramatic.

It can be fun to look at them and get fired up. But at the end of the day, I definitely didn't put too much weight on them. If you read the earlier parts of this section carefully, you know why.

Listen...I know it's hard for some people because there's another side of it that's not fun. People don't like the way they look. I get it. And this is not going to make you feel better, but I do think you should take the picture in your shorts.

The pic should show as much of you as possible, even if you don't like it.

You might feel uncomfortable but it will help you see the physical progression later on. So if it helps you, just remember what I said earlier:

the main point of the progress pic is not to record your physical progress. It's to maintain your attention to detail.

CHAPTER 18

THE EIGHT ERAS OF 75HARD
A USER'S GUIDE TO YOUR 75HARD EXPERIENCE

By the time you read this, thousands and thousands of people have completed 75Hard. To a man or woman, all of them...**ALL OF THEM**...100% at the time of this writing...have said it's been life-changing. In this section, I've included many of the comments that they've made about their experience.

In addition to drawing from my own experience, me and my team have done extensive research into people's day-to-day and week-to-week experience of 75Hard. So this section provides you a basic summary of what to expect.

Please note: every person's experience will ultimately be unique to that person and the realizations each individual has may happen at slightly different points during the program. But there's no question that there are features and benefits of the program that are common to everyone who completes it.

While your exact personal experience won't necessarily follow this **EXACT** pattern, there's a pretty damn good chance that you'll undergo what I call The Eight Eras of 75Hard.

Here they are!

1. DEEP EXCITEMENT AND DISORIENTATION
DAY 1-7

If you travelled back to the year 1892 and visited Ellis Island, New York, you'd see thousands and thousands of immigrants coming from other far away countries and arriving in America for the first time. If you asked them how they felt now that they were in the United States, they would have used two words: excited and overwhelmed.

They were thrilled to be in a brand new land of opportunity and abundance. But it was so new and different that it disoriented them. They loved it. But it took some getting used to.

Based on my experience and the experience of the thousands of people who have already completed 75Hard, that's how you're going to feel in the first week or so.

You are going to feel excited. The reality is, the vast majority of people on Earth don't have the guts or the grit to start 75Hard.

Of the men and women who do, my unofficial estimate is that 99.3 percent of them will give up before they complete Day 3. Why? Because 75Hard is hard. It's the hardest thing some people will do in their entire lives. And as you start out, I guarantee the magnitude of what you are attempting to do will hit you like a freight train.

It will dawn on you that most people would never, ever try to do this. You will realize that this program takes character, enormous effort, and an iron will to succeed. And you will recognize that just your willingness to start already separates you from the average person.

As a result, you will feel some pride. You'll be excited for yourself. You'll catch yourself telling people about 75Hard in person and posting on social media. You'll start imagining everything that you're going to do once you complete 75Hard and become a completely different person.

What's going to stoke your excitement is that, right in the first week, you're going to experience new things.

You're going to discover things about yourself and about life that you never experienced before. You'll feel like one of those immigrants in 1892 landing on New York Harbor and seeing the Statue of Liberty for the first time. You'll be in awe. You might even get emotional.

The first thing you'll discover is how an aching body can feel so good. You'll be sore? Fuck yes, you'll be sore. Yes, even if you're someone who already exercises regularly as part of their lifestyle...you will be sore.

Most people don't exercise every single day of the week—twice a day and once outside! After just three or four days into the program, you'll know you've been working at something big.

That pain will be a source of pride.

And you'll realize something else: the average person lives life like a zombie. They are like the walking dead. Dead people don't feel pain. The fact that you're aching will mean that you are crossing over into the Land of the Living. You are starting to come alive and now you are awake and aware of others critical realities:

You'll begin to notice how many excuses you make. Starting 75Hard and beginning to execute on your critical tasks, whether you feel like it or not, you'll feel like the inexperienced reporter who listens to his recorded broadcast for the first time and notices how many times he says "er" and "uh" and feels stupid as shit. All of a sudden, as if you're reviewing a digital recording of the conversation going on in your head, you'll say "oh, there's an excuse" and "oh, there's another one" and "damn! There are two in a row!" and so on.

You'll notice how many excuses other people make. Once you diagnose the problem in yourself, you'll immediately identify it in other people. You won't just see it in the usual offenders like the loser at work who is always complaining about the boss. You'll see it in people you consider quality, otherwise hard-working human beings. You'll begin to understand that there's an epidemic of excuse-making in the general population of Earth.

*If you have been following along with me for any significant amount of time you'll start to see the world as I see it...and start understanding why I seem frustrated sometimes.

You'll start to notice The Bitch Voice in your head. That's the voice of negativity that tries to rule your mind. The Bitch Voice is responsible for the excuse making. It's the Voice that says "I can't do this because [fill in the excuse]." But The Bitch Voice is guilty of even worse offenses. It's the Voice that tries to undermine your confidence, sow the seeds of doubt, accuse you of being a fraud, and do whatever it can to help you rationalize your way out of becoming who you are meant to be and accomplishing all that you want to accomplish. The #1 strategy of the Bitch Voice is to control you without you even noticing it. But now you are aware. Now you know the Bitch Voice is there, and things will never be the same.

You'll start to be aware of the negativity of the surrounding culture. You'll figure out that you're not the only one who has a Bitch Voice. For every human being on the planet, there's a Bitch Voice inside their head; and most of them are 100% controlled by it, it's the reason lives are wasted, families fall apart, neighborhoods deteriorate, businesses go bankrupt, sports teams go on losing streaks, armies lose wars, and great countries and cultures decay and die. It's the ultimate enemy.

You'll start to be more aware of your time; how much time you waste and have wasted in your life; and you'll start to become more mindful about how you manage it and make the most of it. You'll come to understand that you were never as busy as you thought you were, and that most of the time, you only had to scramble to get things done—or didn't get things done at all—because you mismanaged your schedule and squandered the 24 hours you are given every day. Because of the demands of 75Hard, you will be forced to figure out how to make the most of your day, so that you complete every task and do everything you need to do before you go to bed. When it comes to your time, the mandatory requirements of 75Hard will transform you into a master strategist.

Your eyes will start to be more open to your own weaknesses and areas in your character and conduct that need to grow. Even though this will be humbling at first, you'll feel relief because now you know what you need to work on, when previously ignorance kept you from seeing and ultimately improving.

You'll realize how much you have been operating way below your capacity. Again, this will be humbling. And here's the reality: you may experience a certain level of disappointment in yourself. You'll be smacked in the face by the reality that, for much of your life, you have been underachieving. So you will have a sense of sadness. Regret. Loss. Don't allow yourself to wallow in this too long! Recognize the hard truth that you've half-assed your life, and get excited—because that's about to change!

You'll start to see how much potential you have and what you are really capable of. This is the positive side of realizing how much you've left in the tank up to this point. You'll steadily start to realize what you've been capable of all along; and it won't be long before you push past the humiliation of half-assery to the killer confidence and swag that is created by discipline, execution, and productivity.

You'll realize that so much of who you want to be and what you want to accomplish is directly within your control. You will start to shed the passive, helpless, victim mentality that is so common in the average human being, and you'll start to understand that all the external factors you thought were beyond your control and kept you from happiness and success are really just your own excuses in disguise.

You will become fully aware that the ultimate factor of your happiness and success is you; and you will begin to understand that who you choose to become and what you choose to do is completely within your control.

However, you also need to prepare yourself for a period of disorientation.

When a baby is born into the world, it's a cool thing. But there's a reason it comes out of his mom wailing and screaming. Everything is new and he doesn't know what the fuck is going on!

Going back to the immigrant analogy I used at the beginning of this chapter, when you come to a new country, it's exciting. But it's also completely foreign. You have to adjust to a new language, new culture, and a new way of living.

Sometimes people are overwhelmed and get freaked out by it. That's what it means when we talk about "culture shock."

Well, you're going to experience a certain level of culture shock! And it will be so unlike what you have experienced in yourself and your life that you might find yourself disoriented and unnerved. That's when you're going to face the temptation to give up. (A lot of people say that happens around Day 8). Your Bitch Voice is going to be screaming, "hey, you were comfortable back in your Old Country. This is too much! Let's go back!"

That's when you have to say, "Fuck you. There's no going back."
You have to be like the explorer Hernan Cortes. After he and his men landed on Mexico, he knew they were tired and discouraged and would be tempted to want to sail back home to Spain. So, he ordered them to burn their own ships into ashes!

You get it?

He made it impossible for them to even think about giving up and retreating back to the comfort of the Old Country. They had no choice but to press on. That's the mentality you have embrace. Burn the fucking ships! **ZERO OPTION. ZERO COMPROMISE.**

Bottom line: in this first week or so of 75Hard, you're going to experience excitement and disorientation. You'll experience both of those things because you're starting something brand new. Endure the humiliation of really seeing yourself and your flaws for the first time. Then power through knowing that you're about to blow open the door of your own true potential.

WHAT OTHERS HAVE SAID:

"It doesn't take you many days into 75Hard before you realize it's the small seemingly insignificant tasks that can de-rail progress and need to be given laser focus."

-Matt Sajdak

"75Hard opened my eyes to the fact that, instead of being my own best friend, somewhere along my life I became my own worst enemy and through this program, I'm slowly changing that.

-Jeannette Donofrio

"One of the first things 75Hard teaches you is that you don't find time. You create it."

-Brandon Miller

2. DISCOVERY, DISCIPLINE, AND THE DANGER ZONE
DAY 8-14

It's amazing how focused we get on getting better when we find out we're actually good at something.

Since I'm a car guy, I've always dreamed of the opportunity to participate in a professional race. My great friend Ryan Hardwick does exactly that. He's a professional racecar driver and he currently races in a car we sponsor, 1st Phorm International, in IMSA (International Motor Sports Association) which is the premier racing organization for sports cars in North America.

People who are unfamiliar with racing don't understand what kind of athlete you need to be in order to succeed. It takes almost superhuman levels of focus, agility, and decision-making...as well as great physical fitness and endurance. The difference between winning 1st place and coming in twelfth is a matter of seconds. One wrong steering adjustment, even if you just turned the wheel a fraction of a millimeter, could actually send you crashing into the side of a wall and—worst case scenario—killing yourself.

So when Ryan asked me if I wanted to join him on the racetrack and learn how to drive it myself, I'm not going to lie. It was pretty intimidating. But my love for cars and racing overcame my lack of confidence.

And I was rewarded for that!

After our first couple of training runs, I realized something about myself that Ryan—who is a no bull shit kind of guy—told me later on. I have all the potential to be a great driver. I'm not saying I was awesome at it right from the beginning. Few of us are going to be great at anything we try the first time...this was no exception.

...but If we're going to be successful in life, we have to be willing to suck at something for as long as it takes before we can start getting good and eventually great. You have to be willing to be bad, really bad, before you can be a badass!

But what happened for me was that I decided to commit to a dream, and I discovered that I had the potential to make that dream a reality. Because I discovered that about myself, it motivated me to get even more discipline in the pursuit of my driving skills. I've invested more time heading out to the track and learning more about the mental game and techniques.

You will experience something similar around week two of 75Hard.

You'll discover things about yourself. Cool things. Amazing things you always admired about other people but never saw in yourself.

That discovery will drive you to become even more disciplined.

You'll discover that the time demands of 75Hard actually force you to value your time more and become far better at time management.

In seeing that you really can succeed at becoming the ruler of your daily routine, you'll start to look for ways you can become even more efficient and productive with your time.

Because you will become more time conscious, you will become equally conscious of wasting words—yours and other people's. You'll find yourself not wanting to squander your minutes or hours in pointless conversations. So you'll discover you are capable of being far more direct with the people you talk to. And since you will be honing your discipline, working hard, and getting results, you'll discover a greater sense of purpose and confidence in talking with others.

You'll discover that, mentally, you really can push yourself after you want to quit. So you'll want to push yourself more!

You'll discover that the more you pay attention to the details of your life.

The more commitment you show in executing on the "little things"— for instance, making sure you drink some water every hour or so, turning off your phone notifications so you can zero in our your daily reading— the more "doing the little things" will become automatic for you. Unconscious. Effortless. Enjoyable! And that will motivate you to look for other details you can take control of, to help you become more successful.

You'll discover that you actually like being tested; and that you love the feeling of passing a test.

You'll even find yourself wanting challenges in your life to be harder, demanding that you push yourself beyond your comfort zone! Because you will start to intuitively understand that the harder the task, the further something takes you beyond your level of comfort, the greater the sense of accomplishment. In a sense, you'll start to experience and addiction to what we call **The Process of Test and Triumph.**

For a lot of people, this is a really life-changing and, in a certain way, very enjoyable period of the 75Hard program. It's a time when you are not only discovering cool qualities in yourself you didn't realize you possessed; and you're not only becoming more disciplined; but you're also building momentum. And creating momentum is a huge deal, because riding that momentum is will be really helpful in powering through 75Hard.

Bottom line: you're two weeks into 75Hard and you're starting to roll! You likely haven't gone more than 6 days without "cheating" on your diet or missing a workout in the past. You will be proud of that. Very proud.

But be careful. You have to stay awake and alert. This stretch of days is also a danger zone. Because your confidence can easily turn to cockiness and carelessness.

Yes, you have put together a winning streak. But all it takes is one misstep---one tiny deviation, like forgetting to take your daily progress picture—and guess where that will land you?

Back to the beginning. Back to Day 1.

If you have any integrity at all, you will have to start over from the beginning. If you don't start over...the program will not work as promised.

So, yes: enjoy the new discoveries about yourself. Feel good about earning a stronger self-esteem. But balance that enjoyment and confidence with humility and a commitment to be very, very careful.

Many people who fail, fail in this phase.

WHAT OTHERS HAVE SAID:

"The way you act in one area of your life directly correlates with all of the other aspects. 75Hard has helped me create discipline and stop letting that inner voice (or any other voice around me) dictate my goals and dreams."

-Matty Ode

"Through 75Hard, I've learned how much I used to self-sabotage myself and how little I'd normally follow they with things. Normally by this time i would've had a cheat meal, I would've taken a day off from my habits, but staying on track and following through is what separates average from exceptional."

-Bri Witt

"This is what I've learned: anything you want can truly be reached by putting one foot in front of the other. As long as you keep moving forward while aiming at your goal, you will meet it and surpass it every time"

-Brett Leonty

3. THE EXTERMINATION OF EXCUSES, EXPONENTIAL ESCALATION, AND THE END (FOR SOME)
DAY 15-21

I've always had a great love and admiration for the United State Armed Forces, but I've become an ever greater supporter of our troops because I've become good friends with some of the men who, among soldiers, are the absolute elite of the elite.

One of those men is my buddy J.P. Dinnell.

J.P. is part of a tiny percentage of men who successfully made it through months of brutal physical training and mental torture to become a Navy SEAL.

You know how many people want to become a SEAL? A lot. Because of their importance to national security and their reputation as the best of the best, young men from all over the United State dream of becoming a SEAL. Every year, 40,000 men apply.

After the initial interviews and reviews, though, only about 1,000 men are invited to train for the program; and by the time the training is done, only 1 in 4 actually make it.

Did you catch that? 40,000 apply. 250 actually become Navy SEALS. That's .63 percent.

What most people think is that the men who make up that .63 percent must be gods of fitness, specimens of superhuman physical strength and stamina. And sure, they are in great shape.

But J.P. says that are tons and tons of other men who are in far superior physical shape who never make it. He says that, ultimately, it's not about the man's body.

"It's all about the mind," he says.

It's because those men have learned to take control of their minds that they can get their bodies to do whatever they want them to do—or need them to do. It's their mindset that drives their relentless improvement, their never-ending commitment to become the best of the best, always better than they were the day before.

I'll shoot it to you straight: if you are reading this and you are still in the 75Hard program, you're part of a small percentage that has continued to press on. Maybe not .63 percent. But small.

And if you're still here, you know that something is happening in your mind.

You've been going toe-to-toe with the Bitch Voice for the last two weeks or so, and now you're starting to dominate it. You've initiated a wholesale slaughter of negative thoughts and you're exterminating excuses left and right.

Since you've successfully made it this far, your confidence is really starting to escalate. Your focus is sharpening like a laser. Your work ethic has taken off. You've stopped looking for shortcuts or roundabout solutions and instead are committing to attacking every challenge directly and decisively. In every area of your life, your performance is starting to escalate.

Your standards are continuing to rise.

Your performance is continuing to improve.

You will gain even more momentum.

You will want even greater challenges.

You will crave even harder tests.

You will start to fully realize how easy it is to get results when you operate at full capacity.

You will realize you don't need the support of others for success (and you'll be shown that because most of the people who support you on Day 1 won't be there on Day 21...they'll be onto something new)

Above all, your belief in your potential will start to escalate exponentially.

At the same time, your patience for bullshit will plummet. You won't tolerate it in yourself. You will barely tolerate it in other people.

Now you will see—more than you ever have—the delusions that you've allowed in your own mind, and you will see clearly how most people have accepted and made peace with their delusions, to justify their mediocrity.

You'll come to understand how so many people live in willful ignorance and try to justify the excuses they give themselves for not being who they want to be or living the life they want to live.

You'll see through people. And you'll see through yourself.

For that reason, during this period of time, you'll feel something of a chip on your shoulder. You'll feel aggressive. You might even feel angry. Very angry.

Because you'll feel as if you have been lied to—by the culture, by the people around you, and—most of all—*by you.*

More than anything, you'll experience a fundamental shift in your mindset.

Something will snap. Something will turn. Something will click into place.

Watch for it!

You will stop saying to yourself, "I just want to do my best."

Instead, you'll start shouting to yourself, "I will go as hard as I can until I fail!"

You'll still be physically sore, but by now, you'll just come to accept it. And your acceptance of it will make it irrelevant and powerless over you. The excuses will still come from time to time, but you won't even notice them. You'll ignore them.

This is the time that you will start to really appreciate the 75Hard program—even love it—now that you are experiencing real and undeniable and significant and life-changing progress.

If you make it this far, you will already be a substantially different person for making it this far.

But the reality is, most of you reading this won't make it. And if you do, what is really going to determine whether you experience the full transformation that 75Hard offers is whether you understand that you are just getting started...

...or that by making this far, you've accomplished some sort of "moral victory."

That's what they will tell themselves.

And that's why this time, as incredible as it is, will be The End for some.

Most.

Almost everyone.

Almost everyone that fails...fails here.

If you don't want that to be you, here's what you need to understand: if you have any thought during this time that you've accomplished some sort of moral victory, that is the Bitch Voice making a comeback—and it's only a matter of time (maybe a couple days) before you justify quitting and wash out.

If you are serious about wanting to cultivate the mental toughness that drives higher and higher levels of happiness and success in life, you will have zero interest in moral victories.

The moment that thought even crosses your mind, you need to recommit yourself to winning the battle over the Bitch Voice. You need to double your efforts at dominating that voice. You need to do everything you can to win, not just the big battles in your mind, but the little ones.

Refuse to cut corners.

Don't even think about relaxing your commitment to any of the details or justify the slightest bit of deviation or compromise.

There are no moral victories in 75Hard. Zero.

So don't celebrate them.

...and don't let other people trick you into celebrating them. The only real victory is completing it. Perfectly.

This is the time when you will truly start to experience the power of your mind and see firsthand how it powers your progress and potential.

At the same time, make sure that same powerful mind doesn't fuck you over.

For good or bad, it's all about the mind.

WHAT OTHERS SAID:

"Everybody has their 'reason' for why they didn't do something. 75Hard taught me to watch out, because reasons can become excuses in the blink of an eye!"

-Omar Moreno

"Through 75Hard I have learned that the only reason I have been entertaining other peoples BS is because I wanted an excuse for my own. I no longer have any patience for either."

-Amanda Martinez

"75Hard has taught me that taking action is a decision. Sticking to it is a decision. Following through is a decision. Doing what you say you're going to do is a decision. Putting in the work is a decision. Lastly and most importantly DISCIPLINE IS A DECISION."

-Chris Saunders

MORE MASSIVE TRANSFORMATION AND "THE MOMENT OF MANIFESTATION" DAY 22-28

You like superhero movies?

I'm not necessarily a huge superhero movie fan, but there's always one part of a superhero movie that I really enjoy.

I'll choose the movie Batman Begins to illustrate it.

At the beginning of the movie, we learn that millionaire Bruce Wayne lost his parents when he was a little boy. His mom and dad were shot dead and killed by a mugger.

This traumatic events motivates him dedicate his life to fighting crime and injustice.

For years, he leaves civilization, goes off to the Far East, and is trained in the martial arts by Ra's Al Ghul. He becomes a one-man, hand-to-hand combat machine.

When he returns to his hometown of Gotham City, he knows he can't fight crime as Bruce Wayne. Nobody can know who he is. He needs a secret identity. He needs to carry on his mission as a totally different person.

So at a critical scene in the movie, a group of mafia thugs are engaged in illegal activity, when out of the shadows, he appears for the first time:

Batman!

That's the moment the Caped Crusader shows up for the first time.

That's the day he made himself known to the world.

And when you're watching that scene, you're like, "hell yeah. All his trauma, all his training, all his life brought him to this point. This is who he was meant to become!"

I call that "the moment of manifestation." Or just: The Manifestation.

Superhero movies aren't the only kinds of movies that moments of manifestation in them.

Think of the teen comedy where the awkward, nerdy girl experiences a transformation and suddenly shows up to homecoming dance as a beauty queen.

Think of a sports movie where a team has struggled with selfishness, lack of talented, and internal conflict, but finally gets it all together, and shows up on game day a unified, unstoppable force.

Experts know that every single great movie or television show or book takes a central character and puts them through conflicts and challenges until there is a transformation. They change. And they change for the better! And there is no greater, more bad scene or episode or chapter when you fully and finally see the change.

That's The Manifestation!

Guess what?

If you make it this far in 75Hard, you will experience The Manifestation.

You will have your Moment of Manifestation.

It's different for everyone, but a ton of 75Hard alumni say that their moment came around Day 23, 24, or 25.

That was the day when all their hard work and discipline and perseverance seemed to come to a head.

All of a sudden, they said, "This is who I am."

I am Batman.

Wonder Woman.

I'm a bad motherfucker.

You don't mess with me.

I'm a fucking Jedi of discipline and determination.

When this happens, you'll experience a huge wave of self-satisfaction. You'll see amazing qualities in yourself and you'll know that you earned them. You earned the confidence. You earned the discipline. You earned the toughness. Now, you don't just have those things inside you, you have them in spades!

For this reason, your moment of manifestation will kick off an enormous experience of pride!

But it won't be pride based on nothing but ego.

It won't be the kind of pride that is self-centered or looks down on other people.

It will be pride built on gratitude.

You'll will be so grateful that you have come to realize what the average population doesn't understand: the kind of cheesy affirmations that our culture wants us to tell ourselves don't work.

They don't work because, the truth is, people don't really believe them. They can't believe them!

They can't believe "I am special" because they haven't done anything special!

They can't be happy with their life because they haven't done anything with their life!

They can't "love their body" because they haven't really loved their body. They haven't treated it right; feeding it well, giving it exercise, or making it do great things.

But you will be different.

You will be able to say "I am confident", "I am exceptional" and "I am a bad ass" or whatever else, because you know it's *true!*

You earned the right to believe that about yourself.

That's what people don't understand.

Belief is earned.

Up to this point, when your mind said, "I'm going to do this," you didn't believe it!

Instead, you believed the Bitch Voice. You believed the voice's lies. The voices excuses.

But at this point, you won't be tempted as often to believe the Bitch Voice.

Instead, you'll give control to what I call the "Boss Brain." That brain—and the voice of that brain—is committed to mental toughness and excellence. And over the last 21-25 days, every time you have executed on your 5 Critical Tasks, it's gotten a lot of attention and exercise, and it's gotten strong. It's ready to dominate. It's committed to the pursuit of your own full potential. It's committed to driving you to manifest the person you were meant to be.

The bottom line is, you will feel great about yourself. And that internal experience will have massive effects on the way you relate to other people.

As you think about the typical person out there in the world, you'll realize that they aren't doing anything with their lives, but that you are, and you are choosing to get better. It's not that you will look down on others. You won't, because you'll be so focused on your own self-improvement.

But, to some extent, you will develop a certain detachment, what we might call a "friendly disdain" for other people's opinions. You will feel this especially during your outdoor workout in poor conditions and people are stopping and asking you if you need help when you find yourself out on a run when it 10 degrees out and snowing... like they did me.

You'll also feel this when you drive by the places you used to eat and drink and think to yourself: look at the same old people doing the same old shit (don't forget that was you too).

You won't get angry when people criticize or say stupid things. You won't let it get to you. Because you won't really give a shit. Because you will know what you've accomplished so far. You will enjoy the qualities you've developed in yourself. You will know the kind of person you've become and feel such a sense of pride and satisfaction and gratitude. And if someone points an accusing finger at you or talks shit at you, you won't even really be able to believe it.

"Are you serious?" you'll say to yourself. "Are they really hating on me?"

You might even laugh!

Again, not because you think you are better than they are or that you are somehow a good person and they are bad people. You'll just see the absurdity in them criticizing you.

Because they haven't done the work. You have.

They haven't earned the right to feel good about themselves. You have.

They haven't had their moment of manifestation. You have.

This is a great, great stretch of time in 75Hard, and if you make it here, you will be so glad and I will be so proud of you.

But as always, I have to remind you not to take all this progress and success for granted. You will feel like you are on The Mountaintop, but I guarantee you can still fall off a cliff at any moment. So don't get all caught up in celebrating...you really haven't done shit yet.

Balance your pride with humility. Counter your sense of satisfaction with a re-commitment to being relentless. You could mess up instantly, miss a task without thinking, and it's game over. Back to Square One.

I should also point out that there's a good chance you will also feel *just plain bad.*

By this time, your body will have taken quite a toll. So it will be normal for you to experience a little struggle, a little mental pushback from the Bitch Voice—trying to make you doubt yourself, question yourself, and talk yourself into deviation and compromise.

But regardless of how bad you will physically feel, there's no doubt about the greatness and enjoyment of this stage of 75Hard.

You'll have that moment. The moment you feel like the baddest mother fucker on the planet.

Batman!

WHAT OTHERS HAVE SAID:

"75Hard taught me that I don't have] to prove myself to anyone. If they don't believe in what I'm doing, or want to get on board, fuck them. I don't care. They can get left behind."

-John Mauser

The biggest growth doesn't come from putting in the work that allows you to visually see the physical results on the outside. The biggest growth comes when you hit a plateau and can mentally feel like you're not making progress because you can't visually see it...but then you realize that the growth starts on the inside and works its way out. And so you keep on going!

-Brian Hess

"The lesson 75Hard has taught me is that with consistency I cannot fail!"

-Charles Extrom

5. FOCUS, FEARLESSESS, AND THE FLOW STATE
DAY 29-35

I'm from South County, St. Louis. Since I'm a lifelong Missourian, I grew up in Tornado Alley. Over the course of my life, twisters have ripped through dozens of the cities and towns of my state. Sometimes people have been fortunate and the damage was surprisingly minimal. Other times whole communities have been devastated, leveled to the ground.

When you see footage and photos of places that have been hit by tornadoes, it's disturbing. There's wreckage everywhere. Buildings knocked down. Cars overturned. Power lines knotted up. The mess sprawls for miles, like one massive junk drawer. It's chaos.

But a couple years ago, I saw a photo taken after a city in Southern Missouri got hit by a big tornado. Everything in this picture had been reduced to rubble. Except one thing.

In the middle of the photo, there was a grey stone statue of a Saint. You know? A holy guy who lived sometime in the history of the Catholic Church. I don't know which Saint it was, but what was cool about it was the statue was completely undamaged. Unmoved. Untouched.

And the Saint was just standing there, hands folded in prayer, with a totally confident, calm expression on his face.

Hell had just broken loose around him.

But he was at peace.

The reason I tell this story is because this stage of 75Hard will be one of the most surreal, mysterious, almost mystical and spiritual experiences you may have ever have. It was for me.

As busy as your life may be...you will feel focused.

Even if there's some scary shit going on in your life...you will feel fearless.

While everything and everyone else in your life is twisting and flailing around like a towel in a tornado...

...you will feel as if you've entered a "Flow State."

This is an amazing point to reach.

Your feeling of being in a flow state will be based on three things:

First, it will be based on the trust you've established with yourself.

You've proven to yourself that when you say you are going to do something, you do it.

Second, it will be based on the confidence you earned by doing the work.

Nothing builds our belief in ourselves more than consistent action that gets killer results.

Third, it will be based on a truth that, by now, has fully embedded itself in your mind and heart and will: *"most of my life is within my control."*

You will be amazed at all the factors that you used to worry about, the factors that seemed out of your control, that really aren't.

You'll also fully understand that even the factors that are out of your control cannot and will not derail your happiness and success.

You will understand that your true happiness and success could never have been based on ideal conditions, because conditions will never be ideal!

You'll understand that, the whole time, the determining factor in the quality and productivity of your life is you.

And now you trust yourself to do what needs to be done to become the person you want to be and pursue the life you want to enjoy.

You'll still know there are things that need to change about yourself, but you'll be optimistic and certain those things will change.

You'll know that bad things are bound to come, but you'll just feel fearless about facing them done. You'll feel confident that they aren't going to conquer you.

While you will still need to be alert to the possibility of over-celebrating or screwing things up, the reality is that if you have truly executed the program perfectly to this point, then quitting will no longer be an option for you.

In fact, it won't even be a thought in your head!

As a result, your level of anxiety will go way done.

You *will be at peace.*

I don't mean nothing will ever bother you.

I don't mean you'll never have bad days.

I don't mean that you won't days of discouragement or depression.

What I mean is that you have developed within yourself an inner strength, a foundational source of power that you can rely on no matter what.

You will stand tall in a tornado.

You will be a statue in a storm.

It'll be a paradox.

Not idle, but active.

Not passive, but purposeful.

You won't become some la dee da-rah rah kind of person who irritates everyone with their sugar-coated positivity.

You'll still be driven.

You'll also be fearless.

But it will be a fierceness and fearlessness that is driven and directed by a quiet, steady, powerful force within you.

That's the Flow State! But here's what you need to understand…

The truth is, this experience is incredibly difficult to describe.

In some ways, I can't even fully explain it to you. You just have to experience it for yourself.

But when you do, you will realize that it's like nothing you have ever encountered before.

It's appropriate that I opened up this section talking about the statue of a saint, because the Flow State is almost a religious or spiritual experience.

Every religion, every spiritual movement in the history of Earth recognizes that life in this universe involves mystery.

We can't always take the scientific approach.

We can't always weigh and measure our experiences.

Sometimes we just have to say, "holy shit, I don't know what's happening! I don't know how to put this into words! But it's fucking awesome."

I've actually tried to put this phase of 75Hard into words.

But at the end of the day, I just can't do it justice.

You will just have to do it.

You will experience it for yourself and then you'll understand.

WHAT OTHERS HAVE SAID:

"75Hard taught me that you can say ANYTHING about why you failed... But you're TRULY the ONLY reason it didn't happen."

-Art Monaghan

"Now on the days where I'm dead and would normally rest, I still dominate and do more than someone who is "working hard. That's how 75Hard changed me."

-Rylee Bush

75Hard has reminded me of all the GOOD things that are in me. Strength, empathy, compassion, resolve, focus, discipline. But, those attributes don't come for free. They require work, dedication, and a sharp mind. Those attributes need self-confidence and self-awareness to be genuine, but self-confidence doesn't come from talk. It comes from the walk.

-Jarrod Devore

6. ALIGNMENT, AUTOMATION AND ANTICIPATION
DAYS 36-49

About a 25-minute drive from my office is one of the coolest monuments in our country: The Gateway Arch.

It's not just a symbol of St. Louis. It's actually a symbol that stands for the American drive for adventure and achievement. Historically, St. Louis was considered "the gateway to the West." The explorers Meriwether Lewis and William Clark left from St. Louis on their journey to the West Coast, to see the Pacific Ocean for the very first time.

I want to talk about how the way the Arch was built, because it provides a perfect analogy to what happens in this stage of 75Hard.

Construction crews started building the arch in 1961. It was a huge task. The Gateway Arch is what you call a catenary arch, and they planned it to be 630 feet high. (That's the tallest arch in the world, by the way.) The thing about the Arch is that it was uniquely difficult to build. Why?

The project manager who oversaw it's construction said it was way more difficult than constructing, for instance, a 62 story office building. This is because the Arch is comprised of 142 12-foot long, prefabricated stainless steel sections. But unlike a building, where construction is just put together straight from the ground up, the Arch is curved.

So as these triangle-shaped steel sections were fitted on top of each other, they got more narrow and spiraled toward the top. So as the construction progressed, crews had to use derricks and a scissor truss to make absolutely sure the legs kept steady. You know why this was so important?

If the foundation wasn't kept in the perfect position, if the lower sections angled the wrong direction, even by a one or two inches, the legs would not meet perfectly at the top—what's called the apex.

In other words, The Arch would be cockeyed—probably by several feet—and you would just have two huge steel legs rising up from the ground and never meeting in the middle.

Just imagine the cost—not to mention the embarrassment—of having to start over!

If the crews screwed up at the bottom, even by a tiny bit, it would have had catastrophic results at the top.

So the whole project demanded hard work and paying very close attention to the details. It required advanced planning and disciplined execution of a specific process.

Was it a quick process? Not really. It took two years to build the Arch.

Was it easy? No, of course not.

But the results were fucking amazing!

At the top, the Arch is perfectly aligned. And it's become an awesome example, not only of amazing architecture, but an incredible example of human creativity, industry and—as the "Gateway to the West"— the human drive to explore and discover a new and better life.

Well, guess what?

When you make it to this point of 75Hard...

When you discipline yourself...

When you work hard...

When you follow the process...

When you press on now no matter what...

Eventually, you'll experience alignment.

The desires and dreams you have for yourself and your life will come together with your dedication and discipline to do whatever it takes to fulfill those desires and make those dreams come true.

Let me say that again: your dreams will align with your discipline. Your dedication. And your determination.

And the result will be fucking amazing!

And that experience of alignment will lead to other things.

You know how two people who share a common vision of life and core values just seem to "click?"

When your desires and discipline align, the person you really start to click with is you.

You end up liking yourself, because you are a positive person, you do what you say you are going to do, you trust yourself, and you know that you can depend on yourself to put in the hard work and pay attention to this details. Forget cheesy "self-love." You've become your own best friend, and you're the kind of person that you want to hang out with.

Alignment will contribute to the peace that you began to experience in The Flow State phase. Because there is no gap between what you want and what you're willing to work for, you'll feel more whole. Because you are no longer lying to yourself and making excuses for your weaknesses and failures, you'll feel like an honest, authentic person. Because you are genuinely committed to becoming your best self, you will naturally become a leader of others, motivate them to become better, and by extension, make the world a better place. So you'll feel like a good person, too.

If we really want to simplify it, the experience of alignment is just another way of saying that *you will become a person of integrity.*

As a result of your alignment, many of the things that other people have to push and prod themselves to do will become automatic for you. Excellence will become an involuntary activity.

You won't be as conscious of it. You'll just do it. In fact, it won't even be something you do as much as what you are. Mental toughness will be encoded on every strand of your DNA and your very orientation will be transformed.

You will also start to find that you are linking your successful completion of 75Hard to your long-term success in life. Which is powerful as fuck!

You won't see Day 75 as the end, but as the beginning. You will start anticipating all the things that you want to do—and that you will do.

You'll think about how want to take a new, more positive approach to your relationships

You'll plan new ways to push yourself out of your comfort zone.

You'll take on new tasks and tests and crave the experience of Test and Triumph.

You'll set new dreams that you are so huge that people will laugh at you for them, but you won't be laughing because you know you will do whatever it takes to make them happen.

That's what you can look forward to.

That's what will happen during this time.

You'll experience alignment.

Excellence and mental toughness will become automatic.

You'll anticipate all that you're going to do for the rest of your life.

It's what happened to me.

It's what will happen for you!

WHAT OTHERS HAVE SAID:

"The biggest thing I have learned is that my negative self-talk can only be suffocated by action. At every point when my mind quits or thinks it is over my actions prove it wrong."

-Larry Dixon
"I'd rather start over on Day 1 again as many times as it takes to get it right

than ever go back to the fucking mediocre life I was living before 75Hard."

-Kaili

"Confidence. 75Hard has given me fucking confidence. I don't let anyone or anything deter me from my goals in business, my fitness and my family. I realized just how much my world around me had driven my decisions and had turned me into a pile of useless shit. This whole process has made me realize just how much of those bad habits over time needed to be unraveled"

-Ben Green

NOTE: At this point, the foundations of your transformation have been laid. You've experienced rapid, week-to-week changes, and now in this next major stage, there will still be changes. But the key will not be the number of changes, but the depth and growth of those changes.

In other words...whatever qualities you've created...now you'll start cultivating them more and more and more!

So from this point on, we won't look at things on a weekly basis, but approximately every 10-14 days.

7. EARNED EXPERTISE AND THE EXCITEMENT LULL
DAY 50-63

I have a friend named Rick who is really big into American history, especially the United States' involvement in World War II.

He's read all sort of books about all the majors players in World War II: people like FDR, Hitler, Churchill, Stalin, Patton, and Eisenhower. He's read up on key battles and military campaigns like D-Day, Guadalcanal, and Po Valley.

So he considers himself something off an armchair historian and expert.

But a couple years ago, he was on a Southwest flight to Atlanta when the Captain announced that they had a very special passenger with them on plane. He was a veteran who had been present at the Japanese attack on Pearl Harbor.

As excited as Rick was to have a guy like that on board, he was even more excited when he realized that the dude was sitting right next to him!

He got talking to him and just hung on every word the guy said. This man was able to give a first-hand account of exactly what happened. He saw it all himself.

He heard the blaring cannon fire.

He felt it in his chest and heart every time a bomb exploded.

He smelled the stench of smoke and burned flesh.

He tasted the salt from the Pacific Ocean and the blood in his own mouth.

For this veteran, Pearl Harbor—& World War II—wasn't a subject of intellectual interest. It wasn't abstract. It wasn't theory. It wasn't something he had read about in a book.

Rick was blown away by his insight and understanding.

He knew that what he read from a book could never take the place of the deep and meaningful conversation he had with this man.

This man had lived the history.

He had experienced it in real space and time.

He had earned the right to be considered an *expert*.

And when you make it this far into 75Hard, you will earn the right to be an expert, too.

An expert in focus.

Discipline.

Hard work.

Grit.

Perseverance.

You will have earned your fucking Ph.D. in Mental Toughness.

You won't just be able to talk about it in theory.

You will have experienced it in fact.

It will be a concrete reality in your everyday life.

It's not that you won't have more to learn—there will always be more to learn in life—but you will be to the point that your own personal knowledge and application and experience of mental toughness and its benefits will be so real and substantial...

You are no longer wondering what Mental Toughness is...

You aren't some Instagram bozo talking about it.

You **ARE** living it and could now truly explain it.

And you know what?

You should teach it to other people.

You should share the 75Hard program with them.

You should support them as they work through it themselves.

Why?

Because we love to share the things that:
    1. Have changed our life
    2. We enjoy!

The craziest thing about where you're going to be at this point is that all this hard work & soreness & battles of the mind are no longer something you avoid...they are something you crave.

You will have actually learned to love it all!

You will actually think, "man, when all is said and done, this has all been pretty enjoyable!"

That's what you will tell yourself.

Your mindset is going to switch from "I had to do this" to "I can't believe I *got* to do this."

You'll look back at it as an honor. A privilege.

You'll actually discover what very few people in life have ever discovered: that when you force yourself to go through things you hate to do, you'll come to the point that you don't even mind doing them. You'll even look forward to doing them.

You'll love them!

That's the radical change that happens when you get this far into 75Hard.

And for that reason, you're going to feel a pride that you're one of the few people in the world who has become an expert in mental toughness...

You are one of the few people who have advanced so far that you actually love the art and craft and process of developing mental toughness, and I guarantee you: that's going to create a huge motivation to teach others how they can change their lives, too.

At the same time, this could be your toughest stretch so far. Why?

On a macro level, it's fun. It's enjoyable. Because you are experiencing the benefits in massive ways.

But on a micro level, it's no longer new. It's no longer exciting. It's become a habit and a routine, so in that sense, it's boring.

But that's the point! Remember what I wrote earlier about mastering the monotonous?

When things are new and exciting, motivation is automatic.

But what happens when the excitement fades?

What happens when things become rote and routine?

What happens when boredom sets in?

The average person fails. They abort the mission. They give up goals. They never realize their dreams.

But the mentally tough keep on going and going and going.

This is what separates exceptional achievers from average people.

That's what I've been trying to teach you, and if you have made it this far, you are experiencing it!

This is the most physically difficult phase of the program.

8. GOING INTO GOD MODE
DAYS 64-75

To be honest, by now you don't need me to share much about the experience of 75Hard.

If you made it this far, you are just about done.

You're in the home stretch.

So I just have a question for you:

Do you have a favorite video game?

Teenagers today play Call of Duty, Minecraft, and Fortnite.

When I was a kid, we had a Nintendo; and I loved to play popular games like Super Mario Bros, The Legend of Zelda, and Metal Gear.

One game that wasn't quite as popular and well-known was a game called Contra. It was a war game. You were a soldier who had to blast his way into a secret base and destroy the bad guys. Pretty simple.

Simple, but hard.

There were multiple levels, and each level got more difficult. More enemies to fight. More guns blazing. More bombs exploding. More booby traps to avoid.

One day, I went over to a friend's house, and he was playing Contra. I noticed right away that even though he was getting shot—and hit— by everything from gunfire to missile blasts, he was able to keep going.

Even when he fell into a booby trap, he just bounced back up and kept going.

I was like, "what the fuck? That's awesome!"

I wanted to know how he pulled it off.

"There's a secret code you can enter," he said. "It makes you invincible."

He said, "it puts you in *God Mode.*"

God Mode.

Yes!

"So is there a way to just skip to the end so you can win the whole game?" I asked.

"No," he said. "You still have to battle through all the levels, but if you keep playing and you're in God mode, you'll finish for sure."

What a great analogy for this final stage of 75Hard.

What you will learn by this time is that you can't bypass the battle.

You can't take a short cut.

You can't come up with a hack.

You have to be direct.

You have to be decisive.

You have to move methodically from Point A to Point B.

You have to act.

You have to do the work.

*And you will always have to do the work…..*__FOREVER__

You will always have to be focused.

You will always have to be disciplined.

You will always have to be determined.

You will always have to work to continue to develop more and more mental toughness in your life.

But the reality is, at this point in the program, you will feel as if you are in God Mode.

You will feel bulletproof in your confidence.

You will feel invulnerable to haters and their criticism.

You will feel as if the mental booby traps of the Bitch Voice are completely futile against you.

You will feel like you want things to be harder.

You will feel like you want to be tested more often.

You will feel like you can turn any adversity into an asset.

You will feel as if there is nothing you cannot accomplish.

Two words: God Mode.

You will feel as if you are in God Mode.

That feeling is **NOT** permanent or a permanent part of you.

It will come and go.

But the best way of making it a frequent, near-permanent reality in your life is to take the principles you have learned in 75Hard and apply them every day.

Decide what critical tasks will move you forward toward biggest goals and dreams...

...and complete them.

Without compromise.

Without deviation.

Every. Single. Day.

FREQUENTLY ASKED QUESTIONS

People always have lots of questions about 75Hard. Some of them are questions about the program. But really, most of them are questions about themselves. Questions about whether they really have what it takes to complete this program. Questions about what to do when they hit a brick wall or find themselves a major battle with The Bitch Voice.

In this section, I answer 5 very common questions. But since I always like to over-deliver, I don't just answer the questions. In some cases, I launch into some reflections on life and struggle and mental toughness that will educate you and motivate you.

1. IS 75HARD A FITNESS CHALLENGE?

When people saw the physical requirements for 75Hard, some of them sent me DMs, saying "you should do a mental challenge!"

Let me be clear: this is a mental challenge. Yes, if you do the physical tasks every day for 75 days, there will absolutely be a physical transformation. But the physical tasks are a tool to accomplish a deeper purpose. Whatever health and fitness gains you make are only the evidence that you are undergoing a mental transformation.

More energy.

Greater stamina.

A better body.

These are all key indicators—the proof—that you a developing real mental toughness.

2. HOW IS MY BODY GOING TO MAKE IT THROUGH 75 DAYS OF WORKING OUT TWICE A DAY?

Unless you are one of the elite, elite 6-7 percent of people who already normally workout twice a day, I don't care how fit you are when you start 75Hard. Your body won't be used to the frequency of the workouts. Your body won't be used to not getting a break and taking a day off for almost three months.

So yes: it will take its toll. You will be sore.

That being said, take note of something that James Lawrence told me. (Remember, he's the man who completed 50 Iron Mans in 50 Days in 50 different states.) He said that the body is such an intelligent organism. It almost has a consciousness of its own. After his fifth or sixth Iron Man in a row, he said that it felt like his body just said to itself, "Well, he's going to run another Iron Man tomorrow, so I better do what I can do to adapt and maximize his performance."

So, yes, you will be sore, you will have blisters, you will be physically weak.....but, yes, your body will adapt.

Along with your mind, it will get stronger and less prone to weakness.

3. WHAT IF I DON'T COMPLETELY UNDERSTAND THE RATIONALE AND REQUIREMENTS OF 75HARD?

You need to realize that the key to this program isn't understanding it. **It's *doing* it.**

There are many things in life that we don't understand, but we still know are true.

And there are other things in life we don't really see how they can be true, but someone else we trust says it's true, so we do what they say, and we discover for ourselves that what they told us was 1000 percent true.

But we would never have discovered that if we had tried to understand it first before we acted.

To some extent, you need to approach 75Hard like that.

Why?

Because it doesn't matter if you understand my rationale or not. What matters is that it works. It works really fucking well.

Some of the requirements of this program may not make sense to you (like my zero-tolerance policy on any sort of compromise or deviation) until you actually start executing. When you give yourself over to the program and start experiencing first-hand the process of becoming mentally tough, that's when it will completely make sense to you.

You will only fully understand and be convinced after you execute.

If you want to understand everything before you start, you'll never start.

I'm a St. Louis Cardinals fan. I could explain to you why a game at Busch Stadium is one of the most sublime experiences in all of sports. But until you experience it for yourself, my explanation is meaningless.

As Nike says, "Just do it."

You'll experience the results. Trust me.

The proof isn't in the knowing.

The proof is in the doing.

If you do the program **EXACTLY** as directed you will know you are a different person by the end of the 75 days. ...and you'll love it.

4. I'VE STRUGGLED WITH NEGATIVITY MY WHOLE LIFE. WHAT IF I'M LEGITIMATELY AFRAID THAT I'M GOING TO LOSE THE MENTAL BATTLE IN MY HEAD?

I don't care who you are, you're going to be more tempted to bitch out in the early stages. Don't beat yourself up about that mental battle. It's normal. Press on! The more momentum you build, the less you'll deal with that. Like I just wrote in an earlier question, James the Iron Cowboy told me his body just adapted. You mind will begin to adapt, too. Just trust me.

But let me just also take some time here in the FAQ to share some thoughts on how to fight the battle in your mind.

Here are some things you should know:

When the typical person starts to work toward accomplishing a big goal, the immediate temptation is to think about what they have to give up. And that's why they fail.

Here's what I mean: When they go on a diet, they start fixating on the fact that they have to give up pizza. It constantly runs through their mind. Pizza. Pizza. **PIZZA.** Then what happens?

They end up eating a pizza!

It's like that for everybody who starts out trying to crush a big goal, but focuses on the cost of accomplishing that goal.

- The woman who wants to become an elite level swimmer, but constantly thinks about how cold the water is.

- The entrepreneur who wants to save money to reinvest in his business, but obsesses about how he has to slash his budget and live at a friend's house.

- The man who wants a better relationship with his wife, but always thinks about the Friday nights he's giving up with his buddies.

Everyone one of those efforts is almost guaranteed to fail.

Mentally tough people think entirely different.

They don't focus their thoughts on what they have to give up.

They focus their thoughts on what they are going to gain. They focus on their desired outcome.

- So the woman competing to be an elite level swimmer thinks about how good it will feel to have the Olympic gold medal draped around her neck.

- The entrepreneur thinks about how awesome it will be to sit in his office in his new state-of-the-art headquarters.

- The man who wants a better relationship with his wife thinks about growing old together after sharing a life of happiness and adventure.

Those people will succeed.

Mentally tough people – the people who power through to crush absolutely any goal – take control of their thoughts and focus them on the desire outcome.

They focus their thoughts on what they want.

And they power through...they succeed.

Why?

It's just a law of the universe, a fact of science, and something I've learned again and again in my own experience.

As I mentioned earlier, my friend Ryan Hardwick is a professional racecar driver. Since I love cars, I've joined him on the track a number of times... to learn what it takes to race on that level.

One of the things I've learned is that when you are inches from other cars, it can be insanely stressful. You have to make sure you don't bump into another racer...and you have to make absolutely sure you don't run into the wall.

When less skilled drivers start veering toward the wall, they make a critical mistake. In that stressful moment, their focus turns and they look at the wall. Guess what happens? Always...always they slam into it and the result is a wreck.

They were looking at the wall...so (completely against their intent!) their body moved to turn into it.

Experienced drivers know better. If they sense they are veering toward the wall, they double-down and keep their focus on the track. Dead center. When they do that, they are able to make the correction and keep driving hard.

They were looking at the track. So their body reacted to keep them on the track.

This is a literal, real life example of the unbreakable rule of mental toughness and success.

Your actions follow your focus.

Focus on what you have to give up...and you'll give up.

Focus on what you want to gain...and you'll gain your goal.

You don't have to understand it to believe it. It's just how the brain – and life – works. Period.

So how do you do it? I'll give you three steps:

1. First, you have to reassert the place of authority in your own mind.

That means that when you catch yourself in mid-thought, thinking "Oh, man...I really want a pizza," you immediately say, "Wait. Stop! What am I saying?"

And at that moment, you say, "I'm not going to let myself talk to me like that. I am going to take conscious control and talk for myself and to myself."

You need to realize that you're not the audience in your own head. You're not there to just sit back and passively listen to the conversation going on between your ears. You need to say, "I'm the Drill Instructor, do what I say or I'll kick your ass...(and then deliver the proper message)"

And at that point, you tell yourself, "I can't wait until I'm the fittest motherfucker on my block and all the other Dads look at the ground when I go by...fuck you pizza and fuck you Bitch Voice"

That's when you'll succeed.

But you have to make a conscious decision. You have to take control. You have to reassert the place of authority in your own mind.

2. Secondly, you have to instantly auto-correct the negative thoughts in your brain.

Successful people do that. They take ahold of the negative thought running through their head and they reword it and rephrase it so it motivates them to act and succeed. In Super Bowl LI, when the Patriots were down by 21 points, Tom Brady didn't let himself think, "We're in such a huge hole, we're down 21 points. I don't think we can do this. The Falcons are too much." No! He said, "This is great! We are going to win this game by mounting the greatest comeback in Super Bowl history!"

That's how mentally tough people do it. They might have a thought that is initially negative. It's almost impossible not to. But they immediately auto-correct into something positive.

3. Thirdly, you have to default to what I call your "personal sales script."

They rehearse it and repeat it again and again. What do I mean by that? While we don't do this at my companies, the reality is that a lot of companies use a "sales script." That means they have a presentation that is fully written out and answers prepared for specific questions a customer might have. That's pretty old school and can be cheesy and impersonal, but the reality is, it can also be effective. What does that have to do with mental toughness? Sometimes you have to use a sales script on yourself. If you want to accomplish huge goals, you've got to be able to sell yourself on the idea, and you have to be able to cast the vision to yourself. So when you take control of the conversation in your head, you need to be ready to "pound the points" of your personal sales script into your own head, which means you have to have given them some real thought. These points include:

The vision you have for your life.

The way you have determined – without a doubt –things are going to go for you.

Your goals for yourself that you will absolutely not compromise.

In other words:

- **THIS IS WHO I AM.**
- **THIS IS MY PLAN.**
- **THERE IS NO DISCUSSION.**

Period.

That's the "personal sales script" you need to default to. That's the pitch you have to sell yourself.

That's it. Those are the 3 steps.

Bottom line: people who successfully power through all obstacles and defeat all enemies are men and women who learn to focus on the desired outcome.

They make it their goal to focus on what they want and they take control of the thoughts they think and words they use in order to make that happen.

Like I said:

Those who focus on what they have to give up...give up.

Those who focus on what they want to gain...gain their goal.

4. I'm religious and go to church every day. Does the no alcohol rule apply to taking Communion?

No. Of course not. I understand that Catholics and Lutherans, especially, take Communion every week – which includes a small amount of wine. I would never tell you to go against your spiritual beliefs.

5. WHAT IF I ENCOUNTER A STRETCH OF DAYS WHERE I'M REALLY STRUGGLING?

That's a great sign. Seriously. You shouldn't worry about how badly you are going to struggle. You should take pride in it and love it!

This is something you need to understand clearly and take to heart: average people fear struggle.

They try to avoid it.

They hide it.

They are ashamed of it.

But successful people understand that struggle is part of the success recipe. In fact, it's the first ingredient of success.

It's essential.

It's the engine that drives improvement and achievement.

For starters, struggle is the schoolmaster of success. It's how we learn what we need to do to improve.

If you try to skip over the process and pass on the struggle, you are short circuiting your ability to learn what you need to learn to be your best! And that's going to limit you! Everybody out there who has become hugely successful...

who has made massive amounts of wealth...

I'm talking about the people you look up to, the people you admire, the people you want to emulate, your role models...

...every one of them struggled!

And that's why they are who they are and have done what they've done! They are graduates of the School of Hard Knocks and by struggling they earned their PhD in Domination.

So when you struggle, be proud of it. Go through it with your head held high, learning your lessons with a big smile on your face, and know that sooner or later, people are going to be admiring you, and wanting to hear from you, and wanting to meet you. And that's because of your struggle.

Your struggle is extremely valuable to your success. Don't run from it. Run to it.

The biggest reason struggle is extremely valuable is because it's by working through it that you're going to become confident.

I can tell you that's 100 percent true because I've experienced this in my own life. When things get really hard for me—when I struggle—whether it's in my fitness journey or building my businesses, I have learned to take pride in my struggle.

Because when things get hard, I don't look at it as "Aw dude, things are so hard." That's not how I think about it. The whole process of powering through struggle has taught me to reframe my thoughts and see it from a different perspective.

Now, I say to myself, "life is really hard right now. You're struggling. But here's the thing: right now is when everybody else quits."

"Right now is when everybody else is going to fall behind. Right now is when everybody else decides to do something that's easier or faster or not as hard."

"But **YOU** are not going to do that."

"**YOU** are going to push on."

And guess what? That's exactly what I do. And you know what happens? I usually win. At everything.

I take huge pride in that.

And I walk around with a huge, invincible, cocky swagger. The kind of swagger that you can only have if you go through the struggle and come out on top.

People who have an easy life, people who never do hard things (which is almost everyone you know), they will absolutely never have that kind of confidence.

So when struggle comes, don't fear it, don't try to avoid it, don't hide it or be ashamed of it...

...take pride in it.

LOVE IT.

And really, at the end of the day, all of us want our lives to be one hell of a story. And if there's no struggle in your life, nobody's going to care about your story at all. Nobody's going to care what you did or how you did it.

It's struggle that makes our life story compelling.

It's struggle that gets people's attention and admiration.

There's not one great movie that has ever been made without a tremendous amount of struggle at the heart of the plot. I challenge you to find one. There isn't a single one out there.

Struggle is the most attention-grabbing aspects of our humanity and it's what makes a good book or movie so captivating and entertaining and inspiring.

We are, by our nature, interested in hearing about how other people powered through struggle and overcame their challenges to succeed. *Because it tells us we can do the same thing!*

So if you want that kind of life story that has a crazy kind of energy to it, an energy that attracts people's attention and draws them to you, because you're the center of the story, and they see that you are this super confident, deep and amazing human being who has gone through the fire and come out like a Titan...

...then, like I said, don't fear or avoid or be ashamed of struggle.

Embrace it. Learn from it. Be proud of it and love it!

A FINAL WORD

Now you know all about 75Hard.

I've presented the program that can will help you develop the skills of mental toughness, so that you can become the kind of person who...

...keeps the promises you make to yourself...

...does what you say you will do...

...is focused...

...disciplined...

...confident...

...and tenacious.

The kind of person who literally can achieve anything.

The kind of person who has learned that doing hard things and consistently pushing yourself beyond your comfort zone is the key...

...to ultimate happiness.

So what are you going to do now?

I'll tell you what you should do!

You should refuse to be a Success Zombie. Unfortunately, the vast majority of people who read a book like this one are, in reality, Success Zombies.

Success Zombies are people who are always buying the next self-help book...always flying to the next personal development seminar...always consuming more and more "motivational" products and information...

...and never putting any of it into action.

75Hard is unlike any other product or program out there. But if you want to experience the difference in your life, **you have to actually do it.**

You should execute it exactly like I told you to do it. Remember: no compromises. No deviations. There's no "customized" version of 75Hard. You can't personalize it to your "unique situation."

You should do it immediately. As I said earlier, people who are truly mentally tough understand that conditions will never be ideal. So don't procrastinate starting 75Hard, thinking "Well, I'll start after the holidays when life is a little less crazy." By now, you should understand that the whole point of 75Hard is to teach you to be focused and disciplined whether life is calm or life is chaotic!

Your very first act of mental toughness should be to make the decision to start right away.

Begin.

NOW!

TRACK YOUR PROGRESS & SHARE ON SOCIAL MEDIA USING THE 75HARD APP. AVAILABLE FOR DOWNLOAD FOR APPLE & ANDROID DEVICES.

To reiterate what was mentioned at the beginning of the book: as with all programs that require strenuous exertion & exercise, please consult your physician or qualified health professional before starting 75Hard.